THE 7 BIGGEST

FINANCIAL MISTAKES

MADE BY SUCCESSFUL

ENTREPRENEURS

And What To Do About Them

BRUCE FRANKEL

GREENLEAF
BOOK GROUP PRESS

Published by Greenleaf Book Group Press
Austin, Texas
www.gbgpress.com

Distributed by Greenleaf Book Group

For ordering information or special discounts for bulk purchases, please contact Greenleaf Book Group at PO Box 91869, Austin, TX 78709, 512.891.6100.

Design and composition by Greenleaf Book Group and Sheila Parr
Cover design by Greenleaf Book Group and Sheila Parr
Cover image ©DNY59 / iStockphoto

Cataloging-in-Publication data is available.

Print ISBN: 978-1-62634-437-2

eBook ISBN: 978-1-62634-438-9

Part of the Tree Neutral® program, which offsets the number of trees consumed in the production and printing of this book by taking proactive steps, such as planting trees in direct proportion to the number of trees used: www.treeneutral.com

TreeNeutral®

Printed in the United States of America on acid-free paper

17 18 19 20 21 22   10 9 8 7 6 5 4 3 2 1

First Edition

Dedicated to Claudia and Ethan, whose love and support keep me going and smiling every day. You are *the best*, and I am the luckiest man in the world!

"I know that I have the ability to achieve the object of my Definite Purpose in life; therefore, I demand of myself persistent, continuous action toward its attainment, and I here and now promise to render such action."

—Napoleon Hill

CONTENTS

PREFACE

When I started working with successful small business owners, I assumed, based on their outward appearance of success, that these people must have their financial affairs in order. They lived in nice houses, sent their kids to private school, drove nice cars, and took incredible vacations. We all assume that those nice cars and the expensive clothes and the house in Pebble Beach must mean they're not doing too badly. We assume these folks not only have their affairs in order but have their affairs *optimized*. We say to ourselves, "I'm sure they have the best advisors. I'm sure they know what they're doing. These are very knowledgeable, educated, sophisticated people."

What I realized very quickly was many of them were a mess. Once I started to dig around in their affairs and peel the onion back, I realized they're just like everyone else. They have the same fears and blind spots. They procrastinate the same way we do—putting off whatever takes them out of their comfort zone, just like the rest of us. It was not just that they had a lack of perfection; what I was particularly surprised to unveil was that they were leaving tons of opportunity on the table. These successful people have MBAs and degrees from top universities, but they weren't making their circumstance and affluence work for them to their fullest potential.

Part of the reason is these strategies and their interrelationships are not taught in most business schools. When I pursued my business degree, scant time was spent on the practical application of managing personal finances, especially for business owners. Sure, they taught the classic things about building a business plan and a marketing plan and pro forma budgets. But they didn't teach how these things overlap with your personal finances and what to do about it. We spent virtually no time at all learning about how entrepreneurs can avoid common pitfalls and actually take advantage of being a successful small business owner. The best business schools in the United States leave this void in your education.

As a Certified Financial Planner™ professional, I specialize in working with owners, shareholders, and executives of closely held small- to medium-sized businesses. These people are bright, educated, and savvy entrepreneurs. Most of them are college educated, and many have graduate degrees. Yet I find in my practice that many of these smart people have not done the type of planning and preparation work I will talk about in this book.

I was so curious about why these very bright people leave themselves vulnerable and—worse yet—don't take advantage of their opportunities that I began a process of interviewing many entrepreneurs to find out if they were ever formally taught these topics. I asked open-ended questions to find out if any of their professors in undergraduate or graduate school taught how to optimize value for transition or how to protect their business if things don't go according to plan. I asked if their advisor team illustrated how they can legally take advantage of the tax and labor laws to help them grow and protect their wealth. By far, the overwhelming response was no on both accounts, and some of these entrepreneurs attended very prestigious business schools, including the best Ivy League schools in the United States.

And these people—you, the reader of this book—represent an incredibly important part of the economy. If you are curious about statistics, as I am, you can find your state's profile on the SBA's Office of Advocacy website.[1] The national highlights of the profile include the following (and most recent as of this writing) small business statistics:

1. The United States is home to 28 million small businesses.

2. Small businesses represent 99.7% of all businesses with employees.

3. They employ about 55 million of the nation's private-sector workforce.

4. Small businesses with fewer than 100 employees have the largest share of small business employment.

---

1 https://www.sba.gov/category/advocacy-navigation-structure/research -and-statistics

5. The top three small business industries with the
   most jobs include

   • Health care and social assistance

   • Accommodation and food services

   • Retail trade

6. Most small businesses are sole proprietors.

7. Annual income from sole proprietorships increased
   7.1% in the third quarter of 2013 and totaled $1.2
   trillion.

Given the number of small businesses in the United
States and the number of people these businesses impact
(employers, employees, vendors, and customers), by helping entrepreneurs like you avoid these common mistakes,
I hope to enable you to make an even greater impact on
the micro and macro environment in your life. It's not just
about avoiding mistakes but about helping successful,
hardworking people actually take advantage of the unique
opportunities you may have without even realizing it.

In this book, we are going to discuss strategies that
have already helped hundreds of lives in my business management and consulting work and our wealth consulting
practice. These concepts can help you or people you know.
They are useful at any phase of a business, from concept
to those who have already achieved great success—even
when you're ready to transition one way or another.

However, you can only benefit from this information

if—and this is a big if here—you take action. This is often the biggest obstacle. I can help educate you and provide you with opportunity, but you have to do the work to get educated and empowered to make informed decisions. Like the proverbial horse that can't be forced to drink, I can explain things that are the most logical in the world, but I can't make you take action.

Many business owners decided to start their own business in order to control their own destiny, to make a larger income, or to benefit from legal tax planning. As your business grows and evolves, your finances—and your financial opportunities—will most likely expand. So does your complication and risk; you have more to manage and more to lose. As a small business owner, your personal finances overlap greatly with your business finances.

Please be careful: I'm not saying you should comingle your business and personal finances; that would be a drastic mistake. What I am saying is that what happens in your business affects your lifestyle and your personal life. The art of careful planning involves an integrated design between your personal and your business arrangements. The risk of destroying the family's lifestyle due to poor results or poor planning in the business weighs on most entrepreneurs' hearts and minds. I'll help you learn how to lighten that weight.

This book will guide you through the prominent stages in the evolution of a business, from just starting up all the way through a transition to a buyer or the next generation—and everything in between. Not all of the examples will perfectly fit your situation, but the concepts are useful for every business owner. The point is to make you aware of the common mistakes to watch for as your business evolves.

But knowledge is only half the battle; you must also take action. Your active avoidance of these mistakes is crucial, and this book will guide you through the complicated maze of financial choices and help you overcome the fear, skepticism, cynicism, and—Frankely speaking—laziness that cost you opportunities.

There is nothing more frustrating in life than realizing too late that you lost an opportunity. At my firm, I have people who come to us for wealth and business planning ten, fifteen, twenty years down the road of doing business, only for us to find they have been missing huge opportunities to structure things differently so they can take advantage of their situation. The common reaction is for the person to put their head in their hands and say, "Argh! I wish I had met you twenty years ago!" Another common reaction is "Why didn't my CPA tell me about these things years ago?"—sometimes with a great deal more colorful language than I'm using here.

Of course, I don't have a time machine, but I want to help you avoid the anguish of lost opportunity now and in the future. I want to help you think about these issues in advance so you are ready when they surface. I want you to make the changes now that are appropriate for you at your stage of business and life and to prepare you for the next stages.

This book isn't for huge organizations with thousands of employees and hundreds of investors. It's for the owner of a small- to medium-sized, closely held business. These businesses most likely have less than 500 employees and less than a dozen investors. This book is written for you, the hardworking, perseverant, passionate entrepreneur wanting to optimize your opportunities and avoid the common pitfalls that trip up many.

Introduction

PURPOSE AND PLANNING

"There are two ways to influence human behavior:
You can manipulate it, or you can inspire it."
—Simon Sinek, *Start with Why*

A mentor of mine taught me a long time ago that when most people meet or do business with others, they are very focused on telling people who they are and what they do. If you read the fancy biography at the back of this book, you'll see all the things that represent who I am professionally: I'm an MBA. At the time of this writing, I'm a Certified Financial Planner™. I'm an accredited investment fiduciary. I'm a certified exit planner. But as we all know, all the fancy degrees and designations do not tell the story of who we really are. I'm a son and a son-in-law. I'm master to an Australian shepherd puppy, Milo. I'm a business partner and, in the office, I'm the boss. The kids on my Little League team call me Coach, which is one of my favorites.

My most important title is Daddy to Ethan. And I'm a husband to my beautiful, inside and out, wife, Claudia.

My mentor went on to teach me that most people are really interested in knowing why you do what you do more than anything else. Yes, we all should be able to succinctly explain who we are, what we do, and how we do it, but why you do those things is crucial. Do you really know why you do what you do?

It's not just important to keep you hungry, energized, and motivated to work hard, but it is important for how you decide to plan and prepare. All of your planning work needs to be aligned with the whole you—who, what, and why.

Like most of us, a big part of why I do what I do is to support my family. But in order to feel satisfied and fulfilled in our lives, we have to find more. A significant part of my why is the impact that I and my team make on other businesses and all of the people and communities that are in the circles of influence around each of those families and businesses. Sometimes, that impact requires delaying gratification, because the end result of some of our work is not immediately evident.

Bob Welsh tells a wonderful and touching story about delayed gratification; you can find the video online.

Bob was a highway patrol officer before he became a professional speaker and author. He often worked on Christmas, the holidays being full of events that require police. One year, a woman died in a drunk-driving accident, and he had to notify the family.

When he knocked on the door, a four-year-old girl answered, and Bob's heart sank. He asked her whether her dad was home, and she said no.

"My daddy ran away," she said. "You must be Santa Claus. My mommy said you'd come tonight if I was good."

Bob couldn't bear to call Child Services, so he took her home. She was eventually adopted, and her new family moved away.

Several years later, Bob thought about all the missed Christmases with his own family. If he could do it again, would he give up so much of himself for all the criminals and victims? Would he do it all the same?

Then he heard a knock at the door.

It was late. Who could it be—a neighbor borrowing flour? Carolers? Maybe Santa Claus had come to town.

He opened the door and saw himself decades before—a blue uniform, a badge, and a wide-brimmed hat. It was a patrol officer.

Dear God, he thought. Who has died? His heart raced.

The officer looked up, revealing her face under the hat. She smiled.

"You probably don't remember me," she said. "But you helped me when I was a girl. My mother died, and you took me in for Christmas Eve. I just wanted to say thank you."

If this story and the more effective video touched you the way it still touches me each and every time I watch it, I am glad. Sometimes, we don't really know the impact we're making in our work. I'd like you to stop and ask yourself why you do what you do.

Bob Welsh must have known somewhere inside himself that what he was doing for his community would affect people not just in that moment but for years to come. That was his way of giving back.

However, to take advantage of your opportunities, it's important to explicitly state the reason for what you do. You have to know your core values and goals for your business and personal life, so you can plan for them. This is your why.

When I completed this process, I hired a business coach to facilitate it. I had to be sure my individual personal vision and values were aligned with my business vision and values. It was a challenging process and hard work with the two of us in a hotel interview room about twelve feet by twelve feet. We went through an entire pad of flip chart paper and lots of coffee and ended with a great deal of satisfaction.

Be prepared—I was surprised at how much this was a very emotional process for me. Usually I'm not that way in business dealings. This really got to my core and has inspired me to be even more focused on achieving my personal vision, my individual professional vision, and the combined vision of my company. It is integrated in our company's mission statement:

"Our mission is to empower our select clientele through education and planning to make informed decisions so they can make an even greater impact on the people and causes they care about deeply."

Ask yourself the top three reasons you do what you do. This is a difficult task that requires consideration. You will want to treat the exercise with great seriousness and thought. Start broad, then keep reducing your statements down to the deepest core of your raison d'être—your core why.

Don't trust yourself to remember the exact words or even the general reasons you come up with. Take the time to write it down. Write it down, and post it up on your bathroom mirror and on your main computer screen. Just as it is important to have a written business plan, it is important to write down your purpose.

By far the most successful self-help book of all time is *Think and Grow Rich*, by Napoleon Hill, quoted at the beginning of this book. This is the seminal guide to success as enumerated by Hill's research of the most successful people to that point in history. He assembled the key traits that all of these successful people had in common. Among the most important traits cited by Hill is the habit of making goals and writing things down.

Write down your why to make yourself see it over and over again, until it becomes a mantra. It should drive everything you do.

Your why keeps you centered. Use it to give you strength and persistence to adapt and overcome anything.

Whenever you get frustrated with yourself, your employees, or your business partner, bring it back to why. Whenever you wake up at night, worrying about your business and if it's going to make it or some mistake you perceive you made, bring it back to why. Why takes the focus off everyday turmoil and, more important, takes the focus away from being all about money. Bringing it back to why helps bring things back into perspective.

THE IMPORTANCE OF PLANNING

A few years ago, I received a call from an entrepreneur I've known for several years. He asked me if I would help him and his wife with financial planning. I knew they didn't meet our minimum requirements to become a client, but he's a nice guy, and I like to help if I can, so I agreed to at least schedule a meeting with them. The first step in helping clients toward their impact process is to meet with them and their spouse for a personal assessment meeting. In this meeting, I ask a series of questions to get to know the client and their financial needs and vision and to learn about them beyond their money and finances.

My friend and his wife came into the office without me really knowing what to expect, which is normal for a first meeting. They thought they wanted to talk to me about investing and planning, given they had two small children and wanted to plan for their future. However, once we got into the questions, the conversation, as it does very often, became more about what was going on in their marriage. (With great respect for the licensed therapy community, if a financial planner is doing an excellent job getting to know their clients in depth, they become quasi-therapists.) I realized very quickly they were fighting about money. Well, not just about money; they were fighting over his time.

See, my friend was not spending his incredible energy and time building his business but, rather, was spending a lot of time working with a nonprofit organization he cared deeply about. He was on the board of that organization, and he was spending a lot of time on their strategic planning, working events, and all the things boards do to raise funds and implement their great missions. The problem was he was doing all of this instead of focusing on his own business, growing his income to take care of his and his family's future. To him, this was his way to give back to the community. To his wife, he was abandoning them. Charity starts at home, and if the household is struggling, the income producers in the family need to be focused on easing their own financial burden before expending time and energy elsewhere. He wasn't taking care of things at home first.

Although serving his nonprofit is most certainly a noble cause, he was causing financial and emotional strain in his own house. The strain was to a point where, even though they were putting on a brave face to me, I could see it on his wife's face before she even opened her mouth. My friend, however, wasn't able to see it himself.

It was pretty easy for anyone on the outside to see he

simply had his priorities turned upside down, but he wasn't able to see it for himself. This is not uncommon. When we are in the middle of a storm, we can't see the way out, but everyone around us can see it easily. By not building his business, he was causing the family to struggle financially, which put a burden on everything else in their lives.

How are you spending your time? Is it aligned with your spouse and your family plan?

A well-constructed wealth and estate plan is a blueprint for a family to build their financial legacy. If a couple is ever arguing about matters in any way related to money, a financial plan is an integral part of the therapy that will lead them back to harmony. Just like when you're building or remodeling a house, you do a blueprint. You each talk about what you have in mind about what you envision the outcome will look like. A competent architect will lead you through a logical process to make decisions together as a team. The architect reviews the advantages, disadvantages, and costs involved in creating your vision. You may have to make some compromises along the way, but you are both happy and excited to start building your dream. In the end, your fourth version becomes the final version of what will be built. Then the builder comes in and builds to that blueprint.

Say that if, in the middle of building the kitchen, your spouse happened to be at the house when they were laying out the kitchen island and didn't like what they saw, the builder would remind your spouse that the blueprints do not show the island to be parallel to the counter.

Your spouse might say, "Well, I don't care what the blueprint shows. I do all the cooking around here, and this is going to be my kitchen. Change the island."

You come home and see the island being framed out differently from what you expected. "Honey," you'd say, "we had a blueprint. What happened?"

A gifted architect will step in to be the referee and quarterback all in one. They will work with you and your spouse to remind you of why the original decision was made. They will communicate with the general contractor to see if there are other options to slightly modify the original plan and come back to you with some options. In the end, the blueprint was used as the base to hold all of you—you, your spouse, the builder, and the architect—accountable. Stick to the original plan, or discuss the merits of change. If I were the builder, I'd have both spouses sign off on a detailed change order before lifting a hammer to do anything with the island.

It's the same with financial planning. There is no greater show of love for one another than to go through the financial planning process together, as a team. This solidifies a partnership of equals. It displays mutual respect and supports such important matters as the future well-being of yourselves, your children, and your grandchildren. This process creates the vision for your legacy as a couple and as a family in the community.

A gifted financial planner will be your architect/quarterback to help you identify and communicate your individual and family values system. What we value is where we spend our time, money, and energy. The planner will help you understand where you are today, where you envision being in the future, and the gaps between the two. They will help you understand your options for bridging the gap and the advantages and disadvantages of each option, and they'll guide you to make informed decisions and take action. They will then oversee the building of the plan with the appropriate contractors and vendors to be sure it is built within regulations, securely, and according to the blueprint. As the plan is monitored and maintained along the way, the planner will meet with you to see how well the plan is holding up against internal and external elements that could cause the plan to go astray. The internal elements need to be discussed to determine what caused the change order and what can be done to prevent it from happening in the future. If it represents a change in the original facts, such as income, health, or other major factors, a prudent change may be necessary. If it is an unplanned change in behavior, especially spending and savings, further discussion will be appropriate to find out what has prompted the change.

Back to my friends. This couple wasn't getting along very well, and they were struggling financially. I brought up the subject of the number-one responsibility of a person in a caretaker role: Your first obligation as a caretaker is to take care of yourself before anyone else. You can't take care of anyone else if you don't take care of yourself first.

So I explained to my friend that if he focused on building his business, saving money, and taking care of the home
charity first, he would allow himself to be even more available in the future, to have the ability to do anything he
wanted. He never heard the phrase "charity starts at home"
prior to me presenting it to him.

From the look on his face, he didn't seem to receive this
message very well. When I looked over to his wife, she was
looking at him while nodding her head up and down, with
tears falling down her cheeks.

I told them what I saw: Their financial situation didn't
match their lifestyle. They needed to either cut expenses
or increase income and to start saving for an emergency
fund and for all their other stated goals (college education,
travel, retirement, etc.). I offered for us to set up accounts
and create an automatic savings plan so the money would
never get to their checking account. I offered to help them
create a budget and goals for the business. I referred my
friend to some freelance marketing people I know who
could help him create a plan to grow his business. In the
end, he said he would think about it.

I had no idea whether this had any impact or not. Most
of the time, with our actual clients, I pretty much know
whether they are following my advice, because I meet with
them regularly and ask pointed questions to identify where
they are with their part of implementing our recommendations. However, when I do pro bono work, there are often no
regular update meetings. I bumped into my friend a couple

of times here and there around town afterward, but we didn't get into any detailed conversations about our meeting or their financial plan.

A couple of years later, I bumped into him in line at a popular coffee place. He approached me with a big hug. I was taken aback and asked what prompted the affection. He made a point to step back and hold me by the shoulders and look me straight in the eyes to thank me for that meeting with his wife. He said it took him a while to realize that, sometimes, people have to hit bottom before they take action. The pain has to be more than they can stand. We call that the triggering event. It is that event or moment when something kicks in our brain to change course.

He did finally take action. He built some boundaries around what he was doing with the nonprofit, and he focused on building his business. He told me that his business was growing and that he was making enough money now to cover their expenses and to build the emergency fund I had encouraged. The relationship between him and his wife was much better. She was happier, and they were having a lot of fun together as a family.

The satisfaction I felt from his family benefiting from our work together was exhilarating for me. That's why I do what I do. There's an old phrase that goes something like this: Find something to do that you have a passion for and can make a living doing, and you don't work a day in your life. I encourage you to consider your work and your passions.

AVOIDING PITFALLS

Being an entrepreneur is incredibly challenging. Starting a business is a huge risk, and it requires bravery to take risks. The amount of perseverance required to be an entrepreneur is very rare in our society. Success derives from your willingness to spend the hours and sweat that most people can't or won't. We have to answer to business partners, investors, employees, and customers. We have to be willing to absorb failure and get back up and keep going . . . with a smile on our face. There are innumerable enterprises that fail, for any number of reasons. In order to go through what it takes to conceive, raise capital, start, run, grow, falter, get back up, and grow again, you have to be a strong person.

You also have to avoid the mistakes that less successful companies have made. Learn from their failure. With the number of businesses and the people they affect (employees, vendors, and customers), if entrepreneurs avoid these common mistakes, they can have a big impact on the micro and macro business environment. Avoiding these mistakes will not only keep your business running, but it will also help you actually take advantage of the unique opportunities you may have and not even realize you have.

In general, there are four different categories of mistakes that will affect your future:

1. Mistakes we know we have made. These are mistakes we can seek to mitigate or correct.

2. Mistakes we don't know we have made. These mistakes are time bombs, waiting to go off sometime in the future. We are not aware they are lurking out there, waiting for the most inopportune moment to raise their ugly head.

3. Mistakes others have made. These are mistakes our employees or our vendors have made. We may or may not be aware of these mistakes, which will determine whether the mistake is something we can mitigate or correct or whether it will fall in the time-bomb category. Either way, their mistake will be your expense.

4. Mistaken mistakes—actions we believe to be helpful and advantageous but that are actually harmful. These might be the most insidious of all, since our continued action compounds their impact.

Keep in mind, regardless of who may have made the mistake, it is your reputation and potentially your business that suffers when even the smallest innocuous error occurs.

If you can avoid all of these types of mistakes—or, at least, be prepared and learn how to handle them when they arise—you increase your likelihood of achieving the results you desire. With proper planning, you can not only keep your head above water but sail atop the waves. You can mitigate volatility on the path toward reaching your desired level of success. This is especially important when you are ready to transition on to the next phase of life, whether that's retirement or selling the business to try something new. If executed successfully, proper planning and avoiding the major mistakes of entrepreneurship will enable you to overcome how your business will continue and to focus on why.

Big Mistake #1

THE WRONG
ADVISOR TEAM

"A genius is a person who surrounds himself with
people smarter than himself."
—Andrew Carnegie

Let's say you have a business idea. You've done all of
the classic business planning we are taught at business school or your mentors encouraged you to complete.
You've included thorough research on your market, a
strong business plan, and a laser-focused marketing plan.
You've done an in-depth SWOT analysis. All of your work
tells you to start.

You're probably a pretty smart person, but we all have
to face it: We don't know what we don't know. If we accept
this fact, and we surround ourselves with those who can fill
in the gaps, we are well on our way to avoiding the major
mistakes that can lead to a business failing or sabotaging
your personal plan.

When you start a business, any type of business, you will want to surround yourself with smart people who can advise and mentor you. This is the only intelligent approach for success. Surround yourself with people who are willing to tell you things you may not want to hear, because they are looking out for your best interests, not their own. This is how you build a team with complementary, diversified skills and experience to come to your executive suite (even if that's your garage) to help you and your business.

People often pick an advisor team made up of people like themselves, or they simply don't pick an advisor team at all. Sometimes, they'll try to be do-it-yourselfers and use the Internet as their advisor. The information you can get on the Internet today is unbelievable—both unbelievably helpful and unbelievably dangerous. After the careful planning you've done in the rest of your business, why wouldn't you put that same level of care into choosing experts for your team?

There is also the situation where very intelligent people fail to admit they do not know everything and become complacent. Frequently, even though they may hire professionals to "help" them, the business owner doesn't delegate these functions but is rather dictating to the professional what he or she wants the professional to implement. I advise entrepreneurs to hire your team as I describe above, and obtain their input as to your options along with the advantages, disadvantages, and costs of each, so you are empowered to make an informed decision. If the function requires a specialist who can quarterback the process, delegate the information-gathering and -assimilation process in order to provide the best use of your time—leading your organization.

Now, what do I mean by one of the biggest mistakes made by successful entrepreneurs is having the wrong advisor team? There are four primary aspects of an advisor team. Making a mistake in any of these areas can be lethal to your business:

1. Choosing nonspecialists for specialist positions
2. Choosing friends and family as advisors
3. Failures of communication
4. Using planners who are not planners

YOUR ADVISORS NEED TO BE SPECIALISTS

Quite often, people have advisors on their team who are not specialists in what they're doing. It is, first of all, a mistake to choose advisors who are not well versed and experienced in working with business owners. Many professional advisors start their careers working with individuals and families, whose concerns are very different from a business's. They may not complete additional studies in order to obtain expertise in the areas of business planning and tax mitigation necessary to meet the needs of business owners and their executives. Some may work in large corporate environments, specializing in the issues of conglomerates and publicly traded companies. Most small- to medium-sized business owners do not fit in that category either. The circumstances—and, therefore, the strategies and tactical tools and techniques—appropriate for the large corporate entity are vastly different from those of the small-to-medium-sized businesses or individuals and families.

Working with mid-market business owners requires the professional advisor to have the skills, experience, and expertise to work with the business owner as entrepreneur, executive, family man or woman, and member of their community—not any one role or aspect of their life but the integration of all roles. If an advisor is inexperienced in working with this sort of client, their on-the-job training will be on your time and at your expense.

A perfect example of lost opportunity due to a lack of an experienced business advisor is when I was referred to a couple who just felt they were not optimizing their circumstances. In their case, one spouse is a business owner while the other is a corporate executive. The advisor was doing a fine job working with the family for family planning for a client who is an employee; however, there was no integration into what the entrepreneurial spouse was doing with their business. The end result was years of paying unnecessary taxes and unnecessary exposure of assets to liability and creditors, all of which hampers wealth building and protection. Business owners can only benefit from working with advisors who specialize in working with business owners.

The next level of specialty you will want to consider is if you need people on your expert team of advisors who specialize in your industry or field of work. This is not necessary in every business or industry, but with some businesses these advisors should have specific knowledge and experience working with businesses in your industry. This is how they are best equipped to know the issues and the opportunities, the pitfalls and the risks, with your specific business model.

It is more important for businesses in certain fields to work with a specialist. Health-care professionals in private practice or who operate as 1099 independent professionals have particular issues that should be evaluated in their business and personal planning. Similar to other business owners, when the practitioner gains experience and grows their practice, the issues will become more complicated and opportune. However, health-care professionals like dentists, oral surgeons, ophthalmologists, and optometrists are in businesses requiring high-capital equipment expenditures requiring specialized attention. They, along with anesthesiologists, surgeons, general practitioners, oncologists, and others, face high-liability exposure as well. Furthermore, many of these professionals have partners or shared office arrangements, further complicating their accounting, finance, and practice management due to the integration of multiple practices.

These are also people providing important, mission-critical services to our communities. The community relies on these professionals for their own health, safety, and welfare. This makes business continuation planning, a discussion for a later chapter, even that much more a critical element.

Other professionals who could benefit from an industry-knowledgeable specialist are real-estate investors and real-estate professionals who also invest, themselves, in real estate. These investors have unique opportunities to take advantage of special rules for real-estate investors and those who are licensed. If your investments are heavily weighted in real property, you'll want to educate yourself about additional wealth-building and tax-planning opportunities and consider them for your planning options.

Far too often, entrepreneurs spend the necessary time and effort to be sure they have effective business advisors and mentors but do not ensure they have the proper legal and financial advisors in place early in their business evolution.

Your legal and financial team should comprise a Certified Public Accountant (CPA), a Certified Financial Planner™ professional (CFP®), and a business attorney. This is the strongest three-legged stool of advisors; professionals with these respected designations are all sworn to work as fiduciaries—i.e., in your best interest.

Hiring a specialist is just common sense. Their experience becomes yours, and your business doesn't have to learn things the hard way. Rather than on-the-job training, they bring superior value to your team, your business, and your family today.

FRIENDS AND FAMILY ARE TYPICALLY NOT GOOD ADVISORS

When you start a company, you often don't have a lot of money; the budget is tight until revenue starts rolling in. Perhaps your brother-in-law is an attorney and he offered to help set up your business and offered to do it for a nominal fee—maybe even for free. That's a tempting offer. I understand being frugal. Hey, I'm a finance guy; I don't want anyone to spend money frivolously.

The challenge with this situation is when something goes wrong (and something will eventually go wrong), your relationship is likely to suffer for it, not to mention your business. Remember, sometimes the mistakes an advisor makes are not immediately apparent; sometimes they are time bombs that have been left waiting to go off sometime in the future. Think ahead. What is it going to be like at the Thanksgiving table after the mistake comes to light? If using your friends or family is going to harm your relationship with them and potentially those who are close to them, is it worth it to mix business and personal relationships?

Beyond personal issues, are they the right person for your expert team? Are they experienced specialists in your field? Do they have a process and work in a way that is a good mutual fit for them and for you? Will they work effectively with the other members of your team?

COMMUNICATION IS KEY

Perhaps the most important aspect of picking your professional advisor team is communication. You must ensure a philosophy of coordination and collaboration among your key advisors. I find advisors working in silos. I find advisors who are so full of hubris they actually refuse to work with others. I find advisors who are territorial and simply agree to disagree or who give conflicting advice and are not open to learning strategies or tools to help clients toward achieving their goals. You should all be working toward the same goal—your goals—not for personal points or status.

Think about choosing your advisors as health care for your business. When you have a health issue, you go see the specialist who deals with that issue. However, you have to ensure that your specialists communicate with each other and with you.

In the later years of her life, the mom of a friend of mine took it upon herself to start to see different health-care professionals, who were all specialists. They prescribed medication and, in some cases, referred her to other specialists, who prescribed more medication. At her age and with her desire to gain the knowledge and expertise of each of these specialists, she didn't divulge to one practitioner what the other practitioners had prescribed. Now, let's stop and think about how serious this could be, when there is no collaboration and no one is looking at the big picture. Not only could her various prescriptions cause devastating drug interactions, but the specialists may have been working toward competing goals, undoing each other's progress.

It's the same in business and in comprehensive financial planning. If there is no collaboration among your advisors and you don't ensure that all the professionals are communicating and aware of the others' recommendations, your business and your personal wealth building may suffer. The problems that arise are normally time-bomb interactions, a mess in the future.

It is not uncommon for my clients to report hearing at least one of the following sorts of comments from at least one of their advisors:

"What your CPA said is wrong, and she doesn't know what she's talking about. You shouldn't be working with her any longer."

"What? Your financial planner is dead wrong, I've never heard of such a strategy. He doesn't know what he's talking about, and is probably just making money on you. As a matter of fact, you should just manage your own money, because financial advisors are unnecessary and a waste of money. Just buy a bunch of index funds and be done with it."

"Your attorney is a complete incompetent, and you should fire him and hire my brother."

Of course, they're all right . . . in their own mind. They may even be right within their silo, their limited view of the world. Remember, it's your job to see the wide view.

Now, picture this: You're in the middle of it, and you're going from expert to expert to expert, trying to figure out who to trust and who to rely on to help you make decisions. That's like asking to stand in the middle of a knife-throwing competition—not wise. You need to spend your time building, growing, and managing your business, not refereeing advisors.

Entrepreneurs, you need an advisor team that collaborates for your benefit. If any of them becomes territorial or acts superior to another advisor, you have a problem. If they don't work together as a team, how can this possibly be an optimal situation going forward? Negative interactions will negatively influence you achieving your vision. They'll keep you from your why. This lack of communication may create an internal weakness vis-à-vis your competition. If you have a team with conflicts or operating in silos, you're not helping your competitive odds. It's virtually impossible to manage your business, manage your advisors, and simultaneously be sure you and your family are on target to achieve your personal wealth and legacy goals.

You must insist your team communicate and collaborate as a peer group, on equal footing, and for your benefit.

There is no room for being territorial, scarcity thinking, or power trips here. If any one of your advisors behaves contrary to this principle, red flags should be flying. I suggest you give them one warning and verify they are willing to work in this fashion. If they are not, start looking for a replacement. This is a strategic decision you should make consciously. Do you want to spend your time wrangling petty squabbles or growing your business and spending time with your family?

You'll also need to designate a leader of the team. You're the owner, not the quarterback. Who are you going to put on the field to call your plays? Pick wisely. Every team owner has learned that the most effective teams have specialists.

Billy Bean has become famous for this concept in baseball—known as sabermetrics or moneyball—with the Oakland Athletics. They've taken it to another level by using statistics that sometimes contradict with the conventional wisdom the sport has dictated for decades. They do this in order to find specialists who excel at playing ball in a fashion aligned with the style of baseball the A's play well. They then go out and draft and trade players at each position and role to fit into the style of baseball they plan to manage on a daily basis. This concept has now been adopted by most major sports. They focus on having the right specialists in place at each position based on their franchise players. In football, it's usually the quarterback the organizations will seek to draft and trade for other specialists to surround that position in order to optimize the team's style of play.

It's no different with your advisor team. If one of them is not ready, willing, and able to be the quarterback, it'll have to be you. If they don't respect the knowledge and experience of the other players, they are not going to work as a team. You need to decide if you're going to play quarterback or if there is an advisor you can trust to help play that role.

Your quarterback is not the boss of the team, but they take the lead in coordinating meetings and assimilating recommendations into a cohesive strategy. They need to have the tools (software), knowledge, experience, and personality to be effective in this role. They'll need to be empowered by you to lead the team so the rest of the team appreciates your method and your decisions.

TAX PREPARATION IS NOT PLANNING

Let me first be very clear: The work the vast majority of tax professionals provide their clients is invaluable. Good Enrolled Agents (EAs), Certified Public Accountants (CPAs), and tax attorneys provide great service and incredible added value to their clients on a regular basis. Find yourself a good tax professional who works with you and your other advisors, and you've hit the jackpot. The same should be said of good money managers.

The reason other advisors work together so well with tax professionals for the benefit of their mutual clients is that we do not study and work in the same areas of expertise on a day-to-day basis. We do not spend our time and resources on the same issues, and we study different subject matter for continuing education. In order to keep on top of the moving target that is our US estate, labor, income tax, capital gains tax, and investment regulations and tax code, each of these advisor specialists is required to complete a large amount of continuing education each year. Ironically, however, much of each advisor's work with you will have impact on the other advisors' work.

Consider this: According to the CCH Standard Federal Tax Reporter, the US tax code began with about 400 pages in 1913. In 1939, twenty-six years later, there were still only 504 pages, but then it only took six years for it to explode to 8,200 pages by 1945. It got to over 60,000 pages before the end of the first term of president George W. Bush, and it reached over 72,500 pages by the end of the third year of president Barack Obama's first term of office. The exact total is now apparently at least 72,536 pages as of this writing.

Remember, that's just the tax code at the federal level. That does not address the depth and breadth of labor and tax issues at the state and local level.

I love working with tax professionals who realize and understand that, together, we make a great team because we're able to collaborate with one another. There are some tax pros who have become financial planners. If they have the relevant education, experience, time, software, processes, and proper resources to provide that service at the highest levels of quality and experience, that's great. A financial planner/CPA who has made the effort to become a CFP shows their respect and dedication to the financial planning profession and its important role in helping clients in a holistic approach. You'll want to be sure they effectively spend the time, energy, and resources on continuing education to stay on top of their field in both specialties. Most don't, however, and you will need both an accountant, if you're reading this book most likely a CPA, and a CFP on the team. Even some financial advisors are not equipped to complete comprehensive financial planning for their clients. I've seen advisors doing planning for clients using self-made spreadsheets. There is no practical way they could be properly modeling complex business, personal, and estate planning for their clients.

With my greatest respect to the accountants, tax attorneys, and CPAs of the world, most of them are trying to simply get your tax return done accurately and on time. They will seek to optimize the situation you have brought to them from your previous year of activity. Over the years, I have discussed this issue with dozens of EAs and CPAs. The vast majority of these seasoned professionals have conveyed to me that 70–80% of their income is earned during "tax season," from February 1 to April 15. Therefore, they are under tremendous pressure to produce as many tax returns as their operation can humanly handle in that ten-week period. An overwhelming number of these professionals earn over 80% of their "tax season" revenue in the last six tight weeks from March 1 to April 15. This is due to unprepared taxpayers, late reporting by many investment companies, and the generally massive volume of things done last-minute.

In our building, where I have my office in San Rafael, California, we have a few accounting firms. Every evening during this time of year as I am going home, I see catering companies delivering dinner to these offices. All hands on deck, no one is going home, and they will bring in food and water for their employees so they don't have to go anywhere.

Please don't get me wrong; this is not their fault. The system is set up to be this way. Because the accounting firm essentially acts as a tax factory, it is next to impossible to focus on planning, if they even have the expertise to do so. They are forced to try their best to optimize their clients' situations and keep them out of trouble.

Their knowledge and calm guidance to tackle this incredibly complex area is what you want and need on your team. But don't confuse all of them with an experienced, qualified financial planner working in conjunction with your CPA to coordinate and plan ahead. That's the powerful combination you're looking for.

Keep in mind that your advisors shouldn't cost you anything. Yes, you read that right. Over years of having the right advisors in place to assist you, educate you, and reduce risk, you should save their fee in spades. Depending on your business and their field of specialization, it can be difficult to measure this balance of cost and savings, but over full market cycles in the macro economy, they usually become evident. When you and your business experience both tough times and boom times, the added value brought by your advisors should be easy to see. Some professions bring value that is not easily quantifiable at all. Only you can measure the value this person and their team may have provided qualitatively.

ENTREPRENEURIAL ED

Let's bring this to an example I will refer back to throughout the book, Entrepreneurial Ed, who I will call Ed for short. Ed is fictionalized, but his circumstances are typical of the clients who come into our practice on a regular basis. Ed is a second-generation real-estate investor in his mid-sixties who has taken what his father built and doubled it in the past fifteen years. He and his wife, Edwina, own ten residential properties and are co-owners of a strip mall in the San Francisco Bay Area producing over $750,000 in income annually. This couple has a net worth of $25 million. Ed has an MBA from a prestigious university and prides himself on being an organized and successful business owner, as well as an honorable landlord. His buildings are immaculate and extremely well maintained. According to Edwina, the tenants love him. Ed and Edwina have been married for over thirty years. They have two well-adjusted adult children and a beautiful home in a prestigious neighborhood in San Francisco. Ed is what

I would call a very successful and hardworking entrepreneur. Yes, real-estate investors of this size, whether they know it or not, are entrepreneurs. Ed has a viable business here, with all of the trials, tribulations, opportunities, and rewards of a successful business owner. His business just happens to be real estate.

So what's the problem? I'll answer this question in Ed's own words when he approached me after I delivered a speech to the donors of a large nonprofit organization. As part of that talk I described what I call the five great wealth predators of the affluent, which are particularly threatening for successful business owners. When I finished my talk, Ed didn't waste any time to be the first person to approach me.

He reached out to shake my hand while he started talking: "My father made every one of those mistakes, and I think I am also making every one of those mistakes. When my father passed away, I had a nightmare in dealing with his estate and spent an incredible amount of time and money on accountants and lawyers, only to have to sell assets to pay a huge estate tax bill."

Ed is aware of most of the mistakes he is making. As we all know, acknowledging we have a problem is the first step to addressing that problem. However, yet again, we don't know what we don't know. Frequently, even though a client may have the lingering feeling they are not optimizing their situation, there is even more they don't know—a hidden mistake or a lost opportunity. While you are trying to identify the problem, it continues. It may even grow significantly before you finally take action.

So what should Ed and Edwina do to fix their advisory deficit? They have an EA as an accounting professional. With all due respect to EAs, this client's situation is so complicated I think they need a CPA or tax attorney who understands their business goals and needs. They will want someone who understands, who can collaborate with Ed's other advisors and can help them toward achieving their longer-term goals, both personal and professional. Remember, these two items are inexorably connected.

Ed and Edwina have been paying close to $200,000 in income tax every year; some years more, and some years a little less, but usually right around there. Their EA has never recommended legal mitigation techniques to reduce this tax. Additionally, the EA has not educated Ed about asset protection strategies. In my opinion, this EA is in over their head: Their level of knowledge and expertise do not match Ed's need, and they never suggested Ed and Edwina would benefit from someone who can assist them better. Ed has missed huge opportunities to do something about his income taxes, but he's just kept paying the taxes and paying the taxes, because he's been relying on his EA to be a professional and to give him good advice.

Ed has a business- and estate-planning attorney, but he does not have a financial planner. His attorney and EA have never spoken to one another. His reaction to my talk was that, until now, he didn't know how a financial planner could help with his situation, because he doesn't have a lot of investments in the financial markets. Now, he understands that a comprehensive financial planner is not just for managing money.

A planner who has the knowledge and experience to work in a holistic fashion with business owners will artfully assess the big picture and will recommend long-term strategies and tactics that will help you across most, if not all, of the most critical areas of tax, wealth, estate, asset protection, and transition planning. These professionals are adept at being the quarterback. They help gather and distill the ideas and concerns of the other professionals on your team into one cohesive plan. Through sophisticated planning software, they are then able to illustrate the impact of the recommendations and ultimate planning tools and techniques that are being recommended by your team. This is critically important, given the complexities involved when you have reached this level of success. Assimilating multiple strategies, including several business entities, retirement plans, executive fringe-benefit plans, trusts, family foundations, charitable entities, etc., is difficult, to say the least. When you are provided with this comprehensive view, along with proper education, you are much more likely to become empowered to make informed decisions and take actions that are best for you, your family, and your business.

Now Ed is sixty-seven years old. He wants, and Edwina is insisting, to start to slow down and travel more with

Edwina. As you get older, options and flexibility start to narrow and to become less advantageous. There are simply fewer tools and techniques for us to employ that are appropriate and suitable as a business owner gets older and closer to a business transition. Furthermore, the life stage of the firm itself also dictates what strategies are suitable and appropriate. Tools and techniques applicable for a forty-five-year-old who is five years into their business are not necessarily available for that same owner ten or twenty years later in the evolution of their business. You will reach a point in time, age, and business stage when strategies previously of great advantage have diminishing impact.

Let's take a moment and talk about lawyers. Don't worry; I'm not going to offer any lawyer jokes. A competent collaborative attorney is absolutely important. The law profession is now split into so many specialties you will want to be sure you are heading down the right path with the right professional. As with your other advisors, you will want to be sure they are ready, willing, and able to handle your circumstances and will play nicely in the sand box with the rest of your advisory team.

Also, just as with your other advisors, you will want to understand their fee structure before you engage. I am astonished at the wide range of fees attorneys in our community charge for similar services, so be sure to ask a lot of questions. If their fee deviates widely from the range of others, perhaps they provide additional services for those at additional cost to you—or perhaps they do not.

Sometimes the higher cost–benefit relationship of having a professional who may be more expensive due to the added knowledge and experience, and thus added value, may very well be worth it.

Although not imperative, I recommend you consider an attorney who provides both business- and estate-planning services. At the risk of repeating myself, the overlap in you, a business owner, and your personal affairs is dramatic, and therefore, you could only benefit from an attorney with this dual knowledge and experience. There may be, however, a point in time when you will have a level of wealth and complication that requires bifurcating this role between two professionals.

The trend we are seeing more and more often is people attempting to be do-it-yourselfers with respect to some of their legal needs. When asked how I feel about the use of online legal providers, my usual response is "Caveat emptor." I somewhat understand if you use an online legal provider for simple wills and trusts if you have few or no assets and have no children. However, in most other cases, I will encourage you to use an attorney who can help provide insight beyond what you would consider on your own.

The right advisors will understand your situation, and they'll work with your other advisors as a collaborative team, but there is a danger of overcomplexity. The design of an effectively integrated wealth, estate, and business plan can get complicated. There are some clients and advisors who seem to look for complication, but there is no benefit in creating a situation that is unnecessarily complicated. Quite frequently, this ends up being confusing, expensive to create and maintain, difficult to break apart, and potentially audit prone.

There is also a danger of oversimplifying things. Some compensate to the other extreme and resist the adoption of more and more sophisticated planning techniques, which are designed to grow and protect assets. Avoiding additional complexity due to a desire to keep it simple and avoid spending time, energy, and money means you may be exposed to unnecessary risk and, perhaps, to missing opportunities.

There is a medium in there somewhere. In most cases there is a happy medium between keeping it simple and overcomplicating things. Be sure to not just throw the baby out with the bathwater when it comes to understanding your options. Ask your advisors to create multiple scenarios for you to consider from the minimum they see as imperatives up to the strategies they would recommend to take advantage of your opportunities. They should then help you navigate through these options to make decisions in your best interest.

SELF-ASSESSMENT

Let's just pause a moment. The questions below will help you determine whether you've chosen your advisors wisely.

What is your strategy for selecting your advisor team? _____

_____

Who is on your advisor team?

Business attorney:_____

Estate-planning attorney:_____

Tax professional:_____

Comprehensive Financial Planner:_____

Does each advisor have experience in and understand your unique circumstances?_____

_____

Are your advisors collaborating? Do they disagree or contradict each other? Are they open-minded people who will actively listen to the other team members to learn and appreciate their knowledge and experience?_____

_____

Are you chasing your tail around trying to play quarterback?

_____

Are you putting your hands up in the air because you don't know who to trust and who to believe? If so, it may be time to reassess your expert team of advisors.

I have included bonus material on my website to help you choose a financial advisor. I strongly recommend you start with reading this material before heading down the path of investigating your next advisor. You can also find this and other resources at www.frankely-speaking.com.

We started with this mistake for a reason. Having the appropriate team of expert advisors working in a peer-to-peer collaborative fashion is critically important for your success in business and your ability to avoid most of the other common mistakes discussed in this book. It is vital not only in the early phases of your business's evolution but in the later phases as well. Consider these decisions carefully now and set good strong roots that will support you as you, your business, your wealth, and your family grow. Make good choices now, and these valuable people could be on your team and bringing value to you, your business, and your family for years—even decades. This is the team you want in place to help you in the good times and through the tough times. This is the team you want in place to help you get on track toward optimizing your current circumstances and prepare for the future. This is the team you want in place to help you think ahead and look out for the big boulder in the whitewater-rafting trip of entrepreneurialism. This is the team you want to help you maximize the value of your business in preparation for a liquidity event or transition when you decide the time is right. This is the team you want in place should the very worst occur—illness and even death—to you, a business partner, or family member.

If you begin with the end in mind, your vision for the next twelve months or three or five or ten years from now will be well supported and properly planned—if you have the right team of advisors.

INAPPROPRIATE ENTITY CHOICE AND STRUCTURE

"Any entity—no matter how many tentacles it has—has a soul."
—Guy Consolmagno

There are entire books on the subject of entity structuring, which would go beyond the intended scope of this book and, quite frankly, would put you to sleep. I will tell you this, I see some funny things when it comes to entity structuring, and too frequently, business owners do not understand why they have the entity type or structure they currently have in place. A lot of them don't have an entity at all, which means, whether they realize it or not, they're operating as a sole proprietor.

I encourage you to take your time in researching and making decisions in this area. These decisions can be costly and resource intensive to implement and maintain. The wrong decision here could also be costly to correct or could leave you exposed to liability beyond expectation.

On the other hand, wise decisions in this area have the potential to help you and give you options along the path to achieving your personal and business goals while protecting you and your family from unlimited risk.

I don't want to get too deep in the woods, but let's go over a brief description of the most common entity structures in the United States:

- ☐ sole proprietorship

- ☐ limited liability company

- ☐ C corporation

- ☐ S corporation

The entity choice determines a lot as you move forward—most immediately, what type of tax return you file and whether an entity or you, personally, actually own both the assets and the liabilities, including all potential and future liabilities, of your business.

Before you make any decisions or sign any legal documents, always check with your tax professional and legal counsel to gain their valuable advice and verify anything stated here is current and suitable for you.

SOLE PROPRIETORSHIP

A sole proprietorship is the easiest and most common form of starting a business. In a sole proprietorship, the IRS and state entities treat your business and personal finances as one entity, granting no difference between the two when it comes to financial, legal, and regulatory obligations. All income and losses are reported on your personal tax return annually. All assets and liabilities are owned by you, and the responsibility those inherently contain live with you personally. Of course, be sure you are properly registered to conduct business in your local area and state.

The obvious advantage of a sole proprietorship is its simplicity and cost. You have literally nothing to do to create it. You are automatically considered a sole proprietor if you are taking income as part of a business venture not associated with income you are receiving from another entity as a W-2 employee (i.e., your day job) or other corporate investments. You will want to keep accurate records of income and expenses that are directly related to your business and those that are not. If you are audited, you will most likely be asked for those records to justify any deductions you have been taking for business expenses. I strongly suggest you set up a separate bank account to help keep things separate.

There are several disadvantages of using this as a long-term solution for your business, including exposure to liability and creditors, an inability to take on additional investors, no tax advantages, potential comingling of personal and business affairs, and difficulty for transition planning.

A sole proprietorship does not separate your business

activity and its assets and liabilities from your personal activity, assets, and liabilities. As a result, civil laws see no difference between the two. Why is this important? If, for example, someone decides they were wronged by you in a business arrangement, their attorney will seek to attach any claims for penalty and recompense from the business litigation to your personal assets. All assets owned by you and in community property states, your spouse personally or collectively will be fair game for your enemies' attacks.

In my opinion, a sole proprietorship is a temporary entity choice. If you are going to have a growing long-term business, it is highly likely that other forms of entity structuring would benefit you more than a sole proprietorship.

PARTNERSHIP

A partnership is the result of two or more people coming together to form a business agreement between all members of the venture. Each of the partners contributes to the business venture and will then share profits and losses proportionally to their partnership interest or percentage. Some partners may contribute assets such as cash, intellectual property, or furniture and equipment, while others may contribute their time, knowledge, and experience or some combination of these.

Partnerships are considered pass-through entities, meaning all profit and loss from the business will pass through to the personal tax return of each partner. Each year, the partnership is required to prepare a Schedule K-1 tax form to be distributed to each partner for them to report on their personal tax return.

Liabilities are generally shared proportionally as well; however, recourse debt incurred by the partnership will most likely require each partner to take personal responsibility for the entire debt of the partnership should any member be unable to fulfill their responsibility.

I highly recommend that partnerships create operating agreements among the partners to clarify the roles and responsibilities of each partner. Some partners may be passive investors and not work in the operation in any way, while others may be heavily involved and receive separate compensation for performing these duties, including a regular W-2 salary. Partnership arrangements can take different forms, such as limited partnerships, which do just as the name implies: They limit the responsibilities and control of limited partners, while general partners bear the responsibility to make decisions without the consent of the others. The general partner bears primary exposure to the liability of the endeavor.

The advantages of a partnership lie in its simplicity. No formal shareholder meetings are required, and the business operates and reports to the partners according to the operating agreement. Additional capital contributions may be required from time to time to fund operations or expansion. Partner distributions of profits are completed based on profits, if any, and the operating agreement details.

A distinct disadvantage of partnerships is asset protection from liability and creditors. As mentioned previously, liability and debts are incurred by the partners of the venture, not the partnership itself as a separate entity. When the partners apply for credit, the creditor will require each individual partner to qualify and sign, to personally take responsibility for the debt. In the event of an unfortunate lawsuit, each partner will be personally liable for any adverse judgment.

Partnerships are the sole proprietorships of fractional-ownership structures. They enable multiple owners but do not provide much protection.

LIMITED LIABILITY COMPANY (LLC)

A limited liability company (LLC) is the next rung on the ladder of entity structuring. It is normally used when multiple investors are involved in the business and those owners prefer a greater level of protection than a partnership can provide. LLCs work according to state law. Each state has its particular rules for reporting requirements, disclosures, asset protection, legal remedies in civil court, and other features and restrictions. Some states are more liberal than others. Some require registration if you are a resident and conducting business in that state. There is a wide range of state fees for registering your LLC.

In an LLC, investors are called members of the LLC rather than shareholders or partners. LLCs are often used when deploying multiple entities working in sync with each other in a business, and LLCs can declare their tax status as a partnership or as a corporation.

LLCs are quite flexible, allowing anywhere from one member to hundreds. However, some states restrict certain professions from developing LLCs and other corporate structures. These states require the individual to be personally responsible for the actions of the work performed by the business and its personnel.

The LLC can contract, own assets, obtain its own debt, and generally behave as its own living, breathing entity. However, if the LLC does not have a track record or sufficient assets to collateralize debt, creditors will most likely require the members of the LLC to guarantee any debt obtained.

The main benefit of an LLC is protection from liability and creditors, if properly and legally owned by the entity. The risk of exposure as a result of the activities in the LLC is cocooned from your other assets. I have to mention here that I am not an attorney, but gross negligence is gross negligence, and there isn't protection from bad acts. However, exposure to liability and creditor predatory action is limited to the assets in the LLC. For this reason, I am careful with the amount of assets I recommend you maintain inside your LLC at any given time. More on this later, when we discuss the five great wealth predators in more detail.

For real-estate investors who own many assets, we review the feasibility of multiple LLCs each owning as little as one property in order to limit exposure.

Another benefit of an LLC is the simplicity in setting one up. Most states have easy online processes to create the entity and file your articles of organization. You obtain a federal tax ID number, and—voilà—you have a business entity. Go to the bank and set up your business accounts under the registration of the LLC and its tax ID. Some states may require you to publish the creation of the entity in a local newspaper. You will now contract with vendors and customers under this banner, informing the public you are operating under this entity name and type.

These details may seem like meaningless throwaways but are actually very important. If you are sued and a plaintiff has the ability to illustrate you did not contract, operate, or brand yourself as an LLC or a bona fide—registered and advertised—Doing Business As (DBA) of your LLC, you leave yourself open to a court potentially determining the plaintiff can pierce the corporate/LLC veil. What do I mean?

There are many cases where the defendant in a lawsuit could not demonstrate they operated as an LLC or whatever corporate structure they created. Judges have the ability to look at your situation and determine you acted and operated as a partnership or sole proprietorship rather than an LLC. They determine this by looking at your contracts, your bank accounts, your business cards, your stationery, your website, your chamber of commerce listing, your advertising, and so on, and they decide if you are walking and talking like a duck or like some other species—that is, as an LLC or as a sole proprietorship, for example. The judge will determine if you did so in your dealings with the plaintiff in this particular instance. If he or she determines you did not operate like an LLC, they may determine the plaintiff can attach your personal assets to the lawsuit in order to pay judgments against you and your business. An LLC has the flexibility of determining which tax structure it will follow, either a corporation with S election (see below) or a partnership. In either case of tax declaration for the entity, the structure is also a flow-through entity. The LLC issues a K-1 to the members in order for the members to report the activity on their personal tax return.

Similar to the partnership arrangement, most LLCs should have an operating agreement that provides the details of the roles and responsibilities of each of the members, including ownership interests and corporate responsibilities.

There are some negatives to LLCs. States require annual fees to maintain the entity. Some real-estate investors find it difficult to make decisions about their real estate in a multimember LLC. Multimember LLCs owning real property would benefit from clearly written articles of organization and operating agreements, with specifics on decision-making, including buying, selling, or 1031-qualified exchanges. LLCs without such details find themselves in conflict between members with no facility for resolving those conflicts short of litigation. Such delays or inability in decision-making may cause a loss of opportunity or a loss of significant equity.

To sum up, an LLC is a very effective tool if formatted and used properly. Be sure to dot the i's and cross the t's with your expert team of advisors.

C CORPORATION

When your business requires a more formal structure for working with investors and the public, you will want to consider a corporation. When you register your corporation, by default, in most instances you become a C corporation. In a C corp, the original owners of the firm create shares in the company, which can then be sold to investors. The investors will then own the company proportionally based on the number of shares they own relative to the entire pool of shares created. There are different types of shares that can be created, known as *preferred* or *common* stock. Preferred stock are shares that may include a commitment to receiving dividends before other investors. Different classes of shares can be created to allow or not allow voting rights. There are many ways to structure the shares of a C corp.

A corporation is a distinct and separate entity from any other separately owned entity or your personal affairs and assets. Therefore, it follows that the revenue service will consider your corporation separately for income recognition and then tax the corporation at the current rates and treatment for corporations. The recognition of qualified deductions is basically the same as the deductions you are permitted to take from all other entity forms, from a sole proprietorship to a corporation. There are, however, some qualified and nonqualified retirement and fringe-benefit plans that are allowed in some entity types but not in others. Some of these plans allow for significant deductions or benefits, making this one of those critical points to consider when strategizing about entity structures.

Some of the main benefits of a C corp are asset protection and the ability to relatively easily bring in additional investors if and when needed. If you ever plan to raise more capital through the public or private markets, you will most likely need to be a C corp to do so. This is a relatively easy method to accommodate large numbers of passive investors.

Asset protection is a theme throughout this book—and for good reason. Your personal assets are protected from the activity being performed inside the corporation and vice versa. This additional protection is also valuable when you are involved in other business and real-estate ventures outside your work and ownership in your corporation. Partners, investors, and potential creditors will appreciate that you have created structures that protect their investment and capital from your other businesses. Some creditors will require it, but you certainly save time and show a greater level of sophistication if you walk through the door already prepared.

Later in the chapter, we will talk about multiple entity structures to limit exposure, but this is also a good point to caution you to be careful. In all of these entities, you may want to limit the amount of assets held in your business if you have any concerns about exposure to liabilities. This can be achieved by creating multiple entities but also by distributing capital.

C corporations reward shareholders for investing and staying invested with their firm by distributing profit to the shareholders. If times are good and cash flow permits, the corporation will most likely distribute portions of the profits on a quarterly basis via a dividend. The shareholder who receives the dividend must report it to the IRS on their annual tax return. Dividends have their own tax treatment, separate from regular income to that person or entity. Investors now have the ability to passively invest in your firm and potentially benefit from a current income stream and growth by appreciation in the overall value of the firm and thus their stock in the corporation.

C corps not only benefit from allowing qualified retirement and pension plans but are also permitted to implement nonqualified retirement and other fringe-benefit plans not available in other entity types.

The negatives of a C corp range from record-keeping and tax treatment to transition planning.

C corporations can be complicated and inherently involve a greater level of transparency to shareholders and, in certain instances, public disclosures. A board of directors will need to be seated whose mandate is to hold the executive committee operating the firm accountable. Additionally, quarterly meetings with minutes distributed to shareholders providing details about operations and financial performance are required. This lack of privacy alone may be enough to cause a business owner to choose another route. Following GAAP accounting procedures is another level of complication and, therefore, expense.

The greatest disadvantage of C corps is their tax structure. Income is taxed at every level. The net income of the firm (positive or negative) is reported on a corporate tax return, and if there is tax due, the corporation pays the tax for the corporate activity. The profits now reside in the retained earnings of your balance sheet. If the board of directors approves a dividend, the dividend will be paid from the retained earnings account on the balance sheet; the corporation then pays the cash out of its bank account and sends it to the shareholders holding dividend-paying stock. Now the shareholder has to report that income on their tax return. Let's not forget, in most instances of small, closely held businesses, this is most likely you and your partners. You were just taxed twice for the same activity, once at the corporate level and then again at the personal level. Thanks for playing!

Now let's progress down the path of business success to when you want to transition out of the business and sell your shares. You are fortunate enough to find a buyer who values your company as greatly as you do and makes you a very handsome offer. The offer represents 200% over what you valued the company at and is the cost basis from your shares (I know; I'm being conservative here. You're probably doing even better than that). That's wonderful, and you deserve to be proud of the value you have created. You will now be required to pay capital gains tax on the gain. Most likely, you have owned your shares for more than a year, and the tax treatment will be long-term capital gains. In helping investors, I most often find that they believe the long-term capital gains rate in the United States is 15%. As of this writing, that is true unless your income, including this gain, is over $470,000 for married couples filing jointly. In that case, your long-term capital gains rate will be 20%. On top of that, you would have to pay additional Medicare tax imposed by the Affordable Care Act of 3.8% (see www.frankely-speaking.com for updates on the ACA).

As you can see, the taxes become a challenge. In the illustration above, you will experience triple taxation on the same activity. If I added the estate tax for those of you subject to it, we would have quadruple taxation.

Now, it must be said that much of this is manageable if you are aware and plan ahead. Using tax-deductible qualified and nonqualified plans in conjunction with dividend and reinvestments in the firm, much of the taxation can be minimized. Additionally, it must be said that when you go to sell your stock in your company, you are not just selling the assets, but you are selling the liabilities in the company as well. This may scare off a potential buyer. In those situations, we will explore selling assets such as the brand name, intellectual property, and their customer base rather than your stock. I know I'm repeating myself, but it's that important: Plan ahead, think with the end in mind, and be strategic.

S CORPORATION

If you decide to create a corporate entity for your business, you will want to seriously consider taking an S election to convert your corporation to an S corp. As a reminder, by default, when you create your corporation, you are a C corp. If, after consulting with your expert team, you decide to operate as an S corp, you will want to immediately take the S election.

The obvious question is, what's the difference between an S corp and an C corp? The most significant difference between the two is the recognition of income, losses, and their subsequent tax treatment. In a C corp, the income and losses were retained within the firm. In an S corp, the income and losses are passed through to your personal tax return. The result of this is no taxation at the corporate level, and one tax on the income is created at the personal level only. No double taxation. Also, in S corps the ownership structure is normally divided by percentage of interest in the firm rather than actually issuing shares in the company.

There are certain restrictions on S corporations not present in C corps.

To qualify for S corporation status, the corporation must meet the following requirements:

☐ Be a domestic corporation

☐ Have only allowable shareholders

- Individuals, certain trusts, and estates
- Not partnerships, corporations, or nonresident alien shareholders

☐ Have no more than 100 shareholders

☐ Have only one class of stock

☐ Not be an ineligible corporation (i.e., certain financial institutions, insurance companies, and domestic international sales corporations)

Flow-through entities, especially an S corp, have some very interesting features that, if planned and structured properly in conjunction with the owners' other financial affairs, can be a great benefit. These unique features include the corp's ability to carry tax losses forward and back. This may be helpful when one spouse is a W-2 employee with another firm and the couple's joint income is high. The business has the ability to be legally used to harvest losses that flow through to the personal tax return of the couple, thus reducing overall income, and subsequent tax, of the household.

Again, these things must be planned, but if the opportunity or necessity is there, this can be managed in a strategic fashion for the benefit of the owner.

A word of caution: the IRS form where the type of corporation is decided leads to a lot of misunderstanding. I mentioned earlier you have to proactively make an S election to become an S corp. Many people never do that but operate as if they had. The IRS instructions state that it must be made in a "timely" fashion. Suffice it to say, if you wait for a prolonged period of time, especially if it carries over a tax year, it will complicate things. This is not to say that if you wait, you cannot then convert to an S corp; it just complicates your tax return and stock treatment. This change could adversely impact a future sale of the company.

S corps give you the ability to bifurcate your income between what you are paid as a salary and what you distribute out as a distribution of profit to shareholders. This has to be a reasonable and customary split between the two for your profession. The amount that is paid to you as W-2 income is subject to Social Security and Medicare taxes. The remainder is treated as capital gains and ordinary income to you. The advantage here is you are contributing to the Social Security system for a retirement benefit. The amount distributed does not pay these taxes.

There are not a lot of disadvantages of S corporations for small- to mid-sized businesses. They are pretty simple to maintain, and the tax simplification creates many opportunities for planning. One disadvantage is that some types of executive and fringe-benefit plans are not permitted in S corps.

Here's a typical dialogue I have with a new client:

Bruce: "I noticed you're a C corporation. Help me understand why you decided to become a C corporation."

Client: "I don't know. My tax person told me to start a corporation, so I started a corporation. My attorney helped me with the articles of incorporation, and I filed with the Secretary of State's office."

Bruce: "What was the discussion regarding the tax implications and the options the different types of corporations have for you so you can make a decision?"

Client: "We didn't talk about that."

Bruce: "Tell me about the discussion regarding how the type of entity may impact the types of employee and executive benefit plans you may be allowed to deploy in your business for you, your key employees, and others."

Client: "That never came up."

Bruce: "Did you discuss how many shareholders or other types of investors you are planning for the business?"

Client: "Yes, we did talk about that, and I told him I would most likely be the only investor but that I may take on a partner in the future."

Bruce: "Tell me about your discussion for the future of your company and how you may transition the company in the future. Did you talk about the implications of the different types of entities you may have at that point?"

Client: "No, that is way too far down the road for me to think about anyway."

This example is not meant to insult the intelligence or professionalism of anyone. The client can't know which questions to ask and, unfortunately, he asked the wrong advisor. I'm trying to make a few points here:

First, choosing an entity structure is an important decision. I suggest that it's best decided by involving your entire expert team of advisors. No one knows everything, and because you took the time to research and choose a team of expert advisors who communicate well with each other, you can factor in every relevant consideration in your decision.

Second, entity structuring for your business is not just about liability protection, which often seems to be the emphasis. It includes all issues of tax, benefit plans, retirement plans, business transition, and—yes—protection from personal liability and creditors.

Third, I encourage you to develop a systemized process for making strategic decisions. Included in that process is a robust educational element, requiring collaboration to ensure you are making long-term strategic decisions. Most MBA schools teach us we shouldn't be doing anything that doesn't have a strategic reason. These decisions are the type that can help keep you centered and committed to your long-term mission, vision, and values (your why). Entity structuring is one of those key strategic decisions requiring your full effort and your entire expert team.

When I speak with even the most successful business owners, they often don't know why they're the type of corporation they are.

Now, there are certain professional services and organizations—architects, attorneys, and some medical professionals among them—that are limited in the type of entities they're allowed to have because of certain regulations in their field. As said previously, certain professionals must be personally liable for the work they provide. Your advisor team will help you navigate these regulations.

It makes sense for most businesses early in their evolution to be sole proprietorships. However, operating as a sole proprietorship is, in most cases, a very risky thing. A word of caution is in order. A sole proprietorship is basically you operating as a wing walker, without a tie-down and without a parachute. It's a precarious position to find oneself in. As that company matures and evolves, we need to start talking about what makes sense for the future. If there is immediate risk to assets, a more advanced entity may be warranted immediately.

It is important to realize the full ramifications of making a decision to be or not to be a particular type of entity—if any at all. Frequently, my clients are shocked when I inform them entity structuring could even affect the type of employee benefits and executive benefit programs they're going to be allowed to use. That's why you want to get your advisor team together to talk about what makes sense for you so they can't bounce it off one another.

I might ask, "Are you aware that you won't be able to do things with group life insurance in that type of entity?" or "Do you plan to have a defined benefit pension plan in the company?" We can go on and on of the list of different elements to be considered. The point is there are many factors that must be considered. Be sure you become educated so you are empowered to make good decisions.

A COUPLE OF POINTS OF CAUTION AND INTEREST

Comingling assets, income, and expenses is all too common and very detrimental to you and your financial affairs. I have found even the most sophisticated business owners have this tendency. People operating as sole proprietors and 1099 independent professionals are particularly susceptible to this issue. I have seen owners of professional organizations and corporations comingling all of their financial affairs into their business. They pay personal bills of all sorts through their business and then try to figure it out later. This is fraught with all kinds of complication and liability. I work with CPA firms who have to spend hours and hours of billable time helping clients sort and organize their books before they can even start to prepare their taxes.

The cost alone of paying someone to straighten out your books should make you want to be more organized. Additionally, you risk a judge determining you are not operating as a corporate duck and are therefore personally liable for judgments on your corporation. If something is missed and personal expenses—or "creative accounting"—are used, the taxes, interest, and penalties could be onerous. It's just not worth it. Be organized, keep things separate, take reasonable deductions, take advantage of the tax laws that benefit you, avoid gray areas, and sleep well at night.

HYBRID ENTITIES

There are great opportunities in creating multiple-entity structures that I call *hybrids*. These structures implement a series of entities of one or more differing types to work in conjunction with one another to help you achieve certain strategic goals. Some entities may be employed to hold assets, while others may be the operating companies. Operating companies would have the management, employees, and income recognition, while the holding companies would own the assets. There are numerous scenarios, depending on your situation and your goals and objectives. Be careful not to get complicated just to be complicated. There should be a purpose for each entity and overall structure that is adaptable as your situation evolves over time.

There was a time when we could develop multiple entities with common ownership and could control which employees were reported on one company but not another. The benefit of this was to enable us to follow the rules of that time to deploy multiple tax advantage employee benefit plans that mainly benefited the executive owner of the main company. As you can imagine, some got greedy and abused these rules, causing the Department of Labor and the IRS to restrict this activity. Now, if you create a control group across companies, the Department of Labor will fold the companies together in order to enforce the rules of benefit plans.

The same goes for what are called affiliated service groups, whereby services being provided to the public to a large extent are conducted between companies with common ownership. If these limits are exceeded, the Department of Labor will deem these companies to be a single corporation for implementation of employee benefits. Needless to say, with these great benefit plans come rules to navigate, warranting that you be sure you have a specialist to help with any qualified or nonqualified employee benefit plans for your company.

A discussion here would not be complete if we did not discuss Social Security and Medicare tax treatment (FICA) for people or entities taking in only passive income. Please be aware: You are most likely not paying self-employment tax and may not be creating a Social Security benefit for you and your spouse. I realize a lot of you do not think that Social Security will be there for you, but I find a lot of people are surprised when I ask them to get their Social Security statement in order to complete their financial plan only for them to realize they have virtually no benefit. If that's by design, fine. When I examine appropriate retirement and executive benefit plans to put in their business, they are surprised when I inform them of their reduced options due to not contributing to the Social Security system. If that is by default, it's not so fine.

Registering your business in a particular state can make a difference. Different states have different rules for you to locate your entity in that state. LLCs have particular advantages as asset-holding companies. I suggest you do some research about the costs and the rules of different states. Some are known for more leniency in residency, and some are not lenient at all and may even require management to be conducted in the state. Wyoming is one interesting state that has additional asset protection with charging order status, which could be used for advanced asset protection strategies.

Some wonder why you need all of this asset protection if you just do the right thing in managing your business. We will get into this in great detail later in the book, but I invite you to consider how easy we have made filing a lawsuit in the United States.

ENTREPRENEURIAL ED

Entrepreneurial Ed has a very successful business. Remember, the business nets over $750,000 a year. His personal net worth is over $25 million. He and Edwina are pretty healthy and happy, living a nice life. They travel when they want, where they want, anywhere in the world. Edwina has not worked in over twenty years. At the time of our meeting, Edwina and their daughter were planning a big—and, yes, expensive—wedding.

Don't get me wrong: Ed works hard—very hard. His line of work just happens to be real estate, and his inventory happens to be the units available to lease in his portfolio. Historically, he has researched new property for investment, completed due diligence on the potential property, negotiated purchases, provided capital for purchases and renovations, filled vacancies, managed renovations, negotiated and complied with government authorities, performed maintenance, and provided customer service to his tenants. I'd say he's worked very hard and built up an impressive business. My questions revolve around whether he is protecting what he has built and is taking full advantage of his unique opportunities. Is his structure helping him perform at a high level, or is he underperforming his potential? Will his current structure help him make his impact and leave the legacy he desires?

Here is part of our first conversation during the personal assessment meeting in my office with Ed, Edwina, and one of their children:

> **Bruce:** "I see you have quite the real-estate investment business. Please tell me how these investments are owned and titled."

Ed: "We *own* them. What do you mean—do we have partners?"

Bruce: "No, sorry to not be more clear. How are each of the properties titled? Do you own them as individuals, joint tenants, or another structure?"

Ed: "We own them in a trust."

Bruce: "Great. What type of trust?"

Ed: "Our living trust."

Bruce: "So there is no entity structure other than your living trust?"

Ed: "No. We do have liability insurance."

Bruce: "So you have liability insurance. Are you concerned about liability?"

Ed: "No, but I presume that's why you're asking about entities."

Bruce: "Has someone recommended you create entities?"

Ed: "My dad talked about it before he died, and our attorney mentioned something about it a long time ago, but he said that if we don't have any employees, it's really a waste of money and complicates your taxes."

Bruce: "Is this something that has been on your mind?"

Ed: "Not really, but your talk last week and your questions are making me think about it."

Edwina: "He's been thinking about it a lot since your talk reminded him we don't have anything in place to protect ourselves except the insurance."

Bruce: "Edwina, how do you feel about it?"

Edwina: "I worry about something happening at one of the properties and us getting sued."

Ed: "She worries all the time about it. She wakes up at night worrying about it."

Bruce: "How are these properties managed?"

Ed: "We manage most of them, but the strip mall has a property manager."

Bruce: "Do you pay yourselves a salary for this?"

Edwina: "No, should we?"

Bruce: "I'm not sure yet. Tell me about the conversations you had with your tax professional and attorney about entity structuring and how it can help with your income taxes."

Ed: "We never had that kind of conversation."

In a situation such as this, we need to examine the level of comfort the client has with complication and cost versus simplicity. One mistake a lot of folks make in planning is a motive to save money as well as keep things simple; it sometimes becomes too simple for the situation. This simplicity creates a potential loss of opportunity, too much tax, and unnecessary exposure to liability and creditors. This seems to be Ed's pattern of behavior. Overcomplicating things is not wise either, but we have to decide based on the situation we are working with today, not a situation from the past or a desire to just not deal with it. When you have achieved higher thresholds of success, greater sophistication—and, yes, more complication—is probably going to be warranted. This is not just entity structuring but general planning. I'd like to get you to think of some of these planning techniques on a gauge. On the left end of the gauge, you have done no planning of any kind. All the way to the right end of the gauge is the most esoteric planning arrangement possible. The average person reading this book will most likely be somewhere in between. Remember, there's a middle ground in there somewhere; we just need to work with you to find your happy medium.

Liability insurance is absolutely important to protect your business and your personal assets, but it's not directly relevant to choosing your entity type. I'll just say at this point that in today's society Ed and Edwina are the type of people we say have a huge, bright, neon bull's-eye on their back if someone—heaven forbid—slips and falls and bangs their head at one of these properties. There are many uglier scenarios here, but I think you get the idea. Given their current structure, all of their assets—including their personal residence, their cars, their antiques and artwork, their future income, and so on— are subject to judgments in lawsuits.

It also works in the opposite direction. If something happens in their personal lives causing a lawsuit, their business assets are exposed to this action as well. When you operate your business as a sole proprietorship (a living trust is roughly the same thing), you are operating your business and personal lives in one big pot of stew. There is no distinction that can be made between the two, so the public and the courts will also not grant any distinction between the two.

Ed and Edwina are not unsophisticated people; they assumed their advisors were giving them good advice. However, their advisors did not share vital information among themselves. In addition, Ed did not use a financial planner, erroneously believing that financial planners just manage money or sell insurance.

WHAT ABOUT YOU?

Have you researched whether it makes sense to create a formal entity?

Let's take a look at a hypothetical situation. Imagine you have a real-estate business like Entrepreneurial Ed's. Your son has been working for you in the office, paying bills, and working around the properties. You've been teaching him about the business and paying him a salary. He's making some money, and you have a helper who just happens to be your son. Junior now turns sixteen. Congratulations or condolences, whichever you think is more appropriate. Of course, he gets his driver's license on his birthday—again, congratulations, I think. A few months later, he takes the car to run some errands for you. He sees a friend as they pull up to a stoplight side by side.

They motion each other to drag-race to the next stoplight. The light turns green and they squeal the tires and race down the street. Both drivers swerve, accidentally touching the front ends of the cars, which causes both cars to veer out of their lanes. One careens onto the sidewalk, and your son's car—sorry, your car—flies over the median and into oncoming traffic.

I think you know where I'm going. I'm being dramatic for a reason. This situation is not as uncommon as you think. There are all sorts of versions, but the end result of most of them will be similar. As you know, the legal issues this story brings up are numerous, and not being a lawyer, I won't go very deep. The son being on the clock of the business performing a business function would be more of an issue if there were actual entities in the business and he officially worked for one of them. This would have been a benefit in isolating the repercussions of this incident. However, given there are no entities, it doesn't quite matter; your minor child has caused serious damages, and chances are strong the attorneys who litigate this matter for the injured will seek to attach claims on any and all assets you own. It is highly likely they will be successful. If you've structured your business affairs like Ed, none of your assets—none— are currently protected from this matter.

In practical terms, a court judgment could require assets to be sold, even if it means in a fire sale at the wrong time in the market. Sure, your liability insurance will cover some of this, but that will be quickly exhausted. The current income you rely on for your lifestyle can be diverted to funds set up to settle claims made by the injured. In short, this incident could destroy everything that your family has built.

The main purpose of this book is not to be negative and make you think negatively. The purpose is to help educate you so you feel comfortable to take action and work toward optimizing your opportunities and minimizing your risks. I would hate to think anyone would leave themselves exposed in this way due to fees or fear. Please do not think it can't happen to you. It happens every day, and we can't be so complacent as to not protect ourselves from this potential disaster. This is one of those areas in life where a holistic strategy of a good offense combined with a good defense will be helpful. Appropriate entity structuring is one way business owners can play good defense with regard to exposure to civil liabilities and creditors.

A word about your creditors. I mention exposure to creditors not to help you dodge your commitments. If you entered into an agreement to pay a debt based on true statements relied on to grant that loan, then you should do everything in your power to honor that commitment and repay that loan. The protection I refer to here is for debts across entities or from business obligations to personal obligations. If your business fails and you have not given a personal guarantee on the debts of that business, you most likely will not be held personally liable for those debts.

SELF-ASSESSMENT

Are you sure you understand your full exposure to liability and creditors? Take some time to answer these questions specifically for you.

How susceptible is your profession and business in general to lawsuits? _____

_____

If you are sued in your business, what assets are exposed to a clever lawyer who will search high and low through your affairs? _____

_____

Add it all up and then subtract any insurance you may have for this type of incident or claim.

Are you properly covered for this type of claim, and for how much?

_____

If this happens again, will you be covered again? _____

_____

Is the net amount you came up with something you can pay? _

_____

Are you personally responsible beyond your business assets?

_____

If you own multiple businesses or property, can these be attached to any claims in this incident?_____

_____

_____

I frequently tell clients to think with the end in mind. You've already heard me saying it in this book, and you will hear it again. What is the five-, ten-, and even twenty-year vision for your company, its products or services, its people, and you? What is your vision for how this business will end its life with you? Will it go to the next generation? Will you sell it on the open market? Will you sell it to the employees? Will you just shut the doors or the URL?

Your answers to these questions inform which entity is right for your business. This decision is crucial to protecting your future and should be made with caution and with consideration of the advice of your entire team of experts. At this point, the quarterback of the team should be arranging meetings and distilling the recommendations of each into one cohesive plan. The plan for entity structuring should be clean and as complex as necessary without anything unnecessary. It should be nimble enough to provide flexibility for growth or for downturns. Finally, this plan is aligned with you and your family's long-term goals and vision. It should support your why at every level.

Big Mistake #3

LETTING THE TAX TAIL WAG THE DOG

"The only difference between the tax man and the taxidermist is the taxidermist leaves the skin on."
—Mark Twain

"Taxes—argh!" screams the reader. Despite the confusion and terror involved in figuring out your taxes, this topic tends to be everyone's favorite. Most everyone wants advice on the latest and greatest tax deductions.

Generally speaking, people don't choose their deductions wisely, often because they don't have a strategic plan for their taxes. Remember, you should have a strategic objective for everything you're doing. What's the strategic objective around your tax planning, especially your income-tax planning? But it doesn't stop there. What about estate taxes, the most confiscatory tax in our system? Capital gains taxes can be devastating for families with real estate and other highly appreciated assets. Once the tax man cometh with his vacuum, he almost never returneth with a blower. It's hard to go back and say, "Oh, I didn't mean to do it that way; give me my money back." Remember what Mark Twain said. Yes, ouch.

I'm not referring to a mistake for which you can file an amended return. Remember, each and every single year, once you choose your tax, you're pretty much done with any meaningful change in that tax year. You're committed with your entity structure, you're done declaring your deductions, and you've made the decision about how to allocate your income and expenses. If, for any reason, you learn afterward that you didn't take advantage of other opportunities or you could have benefited from a different structure, it's highly likely it is too late to do anything about it. Furthermore, as the year goes on, your options and flexibility become narrower and narrower. It's of even greater significance with estate taxes. Once you take your hand off the chess piece, your move is done, and you have to start thinking about next year's strategy for substantial tax planning. That's the point. Every year, I want you to think through a five-year plan for your taxes.

TAX DEDUCTIONS

In my professional opinion, most successful entrepreneurs have the potential—if they plan things properly—to save for their retirement simply by saving and prudently investing the money they could save in income taxes over a twenty- to thirty-year period of their business's life.

Entrepreneurs, small- to mid-sized business owners, and most especially 1099 independent professionals tend to take some—what are we supposed to call it?—*aggressive* deductions. I've seen some pretty crazy deductions that will be very difficult to explain should there ever be an audit. We humans have a unique talent for rationalizing and justifying the things that benefit us. The problem is many of these items are simply not permitted under the tax code. Other items are permitted if the taxpayer keeps good records and can justify the business need and use. Unfortunately, most of us do not do a very good job of keeping records to support the business claim. Now, of course, there are bona fide deductions from running your business. You have to operate your business, you have to buy certain things, and you have to incur expenses. But you have to follow the law as well and keep good records in order to not have any problems with the tax authorities.

If we step back a moment and think about things a bit more strategically, which is my consistent message to you throughout this book, there are three main categories for you to consider when you plan your income tax strategy to benefit your business and, ultimately, you and your family.

- ☐ General business expenses for operations and growth

- ☐ Expenses for equipment, machinery, vehicles

- ☐ Your retirement plan for you and your employees

If you are in the fortunate position to take advantage of all three of these areas, then go for it. Quite often I find clients taking deductions without being fully educated on other options for long-term tax planning; they're just thinking about the current benefit. Strategic tax planning is a long-term proposition depending on your current and anticipated cash flow needs, desire to pay the tax later versus now, and your other investment strategies.

Let's look at the life cycle of different types of deductions. In some cases, it's sort of a short and sad life. Far too often business owners use—and abuse—deductions for the short-lived benefit of one year, helping pay a little bit less to the government (in some cases, a lot less) that year. As soon as they are finished with that deduction, they will move on in search of the next deduction for the next year. Sure, sometimes we have a few good ones we continually use many times in a year, but beyond the initial gratification, there is really no long-term relationship with or commitment to the deduction beyond that one year of benefit.

The point here is there are other options that may have a longer life and a longer benefit for your business or personal taxes. Let's take a closer look at the three categories and see how they can benefit you.

General business expenses for operations and growth

General business expenses is a broad category that includes every noncapitalized expense you incur to supply, tool, manufacture, market, distribute, operate, and manage your business in a given year. We add all that up and take that expense as a deduction to your income for the year. Your CPA agrees with the deductions and puts them on your business return. You got the deduction and achieved the goal to lower your income on paper and pay less in tax *this* year. Everybody is happy.

This area tends to be the primary and, in some cases, entire focus of people, most especially business owners. These entrepreneurs often seek to take deductions for everything possible. They are motivated by the immediate gratification of the deduction and the utility of the expense immediately—sort of like having your cake and eating it too. The motivation for tax deductions often rationalizes spending beyond our needs. Some of these businesspeople say to themselves, "I can buy a nicer computer, desk, cabinet, printer, or the latest gadget because I'm going to get a tax deduction." It's sort of a discount or a sale, and who doesn't love a great deal? And it's not just things; they'll say, "I can spend more money on marketing. I can have a nicer website. I can upgrade my technology." The temptation to spend more money grows, because we have this little guy sitting on one shoulder saying, "I can spend a little more because I'm getting a deduction for it, so I'm really not spending that much." I think many of us quickly calculate the difference in our heads while we're making these decisions that it's not really costing as much as we're spending. It's amazing how the human brain can rationalize just about anything we really want to rationalize.

I see incredible creativity with my clients for these deductions. Owners of closely held businesses and independent contractors seem to come up with every possible reason for deductions, just for the sake of taking deductions. The twists and turns result in the tax tail wagging the dog: The purpose is maximizing deductions for the current tax year rather than determining the most effective and beneficial long-term tax strategy. Most of the time, the net result of it all is simply not worth the effort or the risk of the IRS disagreeing with you. Frequently, the taxpayer ends up running into the alternative minimum tax (AMT) anyway and has to pay their minimum tax based on their income regardless. Also, have you ever been through an audit? It's not fun, but it is expensive.

When you spend money, even if you deduct it, you're still spending the money. Don't forget, your author is a Certified Financial Planner™ professional; I don't want you spending money frivolously. Capital is capital and should be used for its highest and best use at the moment. Be careful how much money you spend, even if you're getting a deduction. It isn't how much money you are "saving," don't get me wrong; that is important, but it is much more important to evaluate how much money you get to keep in the long run. This is what affects the net cash flow of your business and, ultimately, your personal cash flow. Again, I remind you to think with the end in mind; one of the primary metrics we look at when evaluating a firm for sale or acquisition by a client is the free cash flow of that business. If you extract the cash flow out of the business annually to take current deductions above and beyond necessary expenses to run your business, you are skewing your income statement toward less profitability. This may be the most important point of this chapter. If you intend to transfer your business in some sort of sale, you will have a difficult time justifying your reduced profitability. You won't be able to say, "Well, I was very aggressive with my deductions to pay less tax. My business is really much more profitable than it looks." That won't work. Choose your deductions wisely. Read on and you'll learn how. Bear with me here as I go through some numbers to illustrate a point.

So what is the life of this type of deduction?

Let's take a $10,000 expense for general expenses. This is not capital equipment over $1,000 requiring a depreciation schedule. You make ongoing non-mission-critical investment in your business as "operating" expenses. If you are in a 40% combined tax bracket, this $10,000 deduction will net you a $4,000 reduction in your tax liability for that tax year. Let's assume you take that $4,000 and invest it in an all-equity-growth-oriented portfolio. You weren't going to spend that savings, were you?

For our hypothetical illustration, incorporating both a bull market and a market bubble burst, we will assume annual returns in the S&P 500 index from 2005 to 2014. At the end of the nine-year period, your $4,000 would be worth a whopping $6,597.

Hopefully, the investment you made in your business (yes, your annual expenses are a way of choosing to continue to invest in your business) led to massive growth or cost savings in the business. If it was invested wisely, you should have benefited from the utility of the investment. If this expense was for technology or equipment, that equipment is likely out of date by now and will have to be replaced again, thus repeating this expense every few years.

To review, your $10,000 investment is worth $6,597 after ten years. That is a return of −34.03% over the ten-year period. The problem here is you take an immediate 60% loss on your cash flow the second you decide to spend those funds. If you need to and it is mission critical to your business, so be it. When you have choices about the use of your capital, be careful not to spend or invest simply to get current-year tax deductions.

The bottom line of this type of deduction is that it only benefits you on your tax return for the single year you made the deduction. It is not an ongoing program to give you substantial deductions for several years. If deductions are taking advantage of so-called loopholes in the tax code, these are the first items on the list to be eliminated in any tax reform that will eventually happen. If these are mission-critical expenses and deductions to properly operate and grow your business, then by all means spend to your previously planned budget. Just watch for falling into the traps discussed here. Don't forget, each year, you have to justify these expenses, get your deduction, and then you have to start doing it for the next year and so on. It is my hope you at least optimize this strategy and invest the savings, not just spend it.

Expenses for equipment, machinery, vehicles

In the category above, we were only discussing regular operational expenses. In this section, let's talk about deductions for larger expenses that normally fall under capital expenses. These are items the IRS has determined have a longer useful life than the single year in the examples above. Therefore, you are required to expense these items over several years. There are current proposals to change this rule and allow immediate expensing of all capital items. These are things like equipment for you or your team to perform a job function, machinery needed for manufacturing, and vehicles required to transport people or products in the delivery or processes necessary to complete your product or services. The biggest mistake I see in practice is the business owner buying or leasing more than they need to complete the task at hand. How about a sexy deduction—a car? The purchase or lease of a car for business purposes has become more and more popular in recent years. I'm not going to get into the rules of what legally constitutes a bona fide company car but will restrict this discussion to the deduction so we can stay on topic.

For the purposes of this example, we will assume the car is $10,000 and paid for in cash. I know that is not a lot of money for a car, especially when we have that little guy in our head telling us we can buy a nicer car because we are getting a deduction. I've kept the price at $10,000 to keep our examples in each of the categories comparable.

As we all know, as soon as you drive the car off the lot, it begins to lose value; it depreciates. You should now realize that you took a deduction for a depreciating asset. In my opinion, taking deductions for depreciating assets is not the most efficient use of cash flow. As you will hopefully see by the end of this chapter, you need to decide your highest and best use of your cash flow as it pertains to your long-term tax strategy.

Bottom line: Choose your deductions and your spending wisely—strategically. If you do not need to have that nice of a car, then save those funds for something else. Once you make the decisions about how you want to use your cash flow and implement it, the capital is gone and may very well represent an opportunity cost. Once that cash is gone, it's gone. I want you to be especially careful when deploying liquid assets, most especially if you are converting them to illiquid assets. These types of decisions should be made with great care.

So what is the life of this type of deduction?

Staying in our 40% combined tax bracket, a $10,000 income deduction will net you a $4,000 tax liability reduction. But this time, we have to take depreciation into account. We'll take your brand-new shiny $10,000 asset, we'll depreciate it according to the IRS auto depreciation schedule, and then we'll invest your $4,000 tax deduction as we did in the previous example. Remember, according to this financial planner, your humble author, that tax savings isn't there for you to spend; it's there for you to invest in your future by reinvesting in your business, your employees, or your retirement plan. Otherwise, we would need to subtract that opportunity cost from the gain or loss of your income deduction in order to illustrate the example without saving and investing the tax reduction but rather show you spending the entire amount.

Again, for our hypothetical illustration, we will assume annual returns in the S&P 500 index and use the annual returns from 2005 to 2014. At the end of the nine-year period, your $10,000 depreciating asset and your $4,000 would be worth a whopping $10,338. That represents a return of 3.38% over the nine-year period, a 0.338% annual return on your capital. Of that $10,338 in total assets you have from this endeavor, $6,597 is in your investment account and $3,741 is in the value of the automobile at the end of the nine-year period.

Your retirement plan

Let's now look at the third major category of expenses for a closely held business and its owners: a retirement plan. Depending on your business and personal situations, there is a wide range of plan types you can deploy in the business, from a SEP IRA (a simplified employee pension individual retirement arrangement) all the way to a defined benefit pension plan and several other qualified plans and hybrid plans. But we are going to keep it simple for illustration purposes.

If you use a portion of your cash flow to start a retirement plan—say, the familiar $10,000—we get the same deduction as in the previous examples. Hopefully, it appreciates, as opposed to the previous examples, where the net impact of your deduction did nothing more for you over the life of the asset. If you invest in a retirement plan, over time, ten or twenty years, it will follow the market, which has historically always gained value.

So what is the life of this type of deduction?

This is the same investment as the last two scenarios—$10,000—but this time, you get the benefit of both the amount of cash flow invested and the deduction. The $10,000 is in one account for the retirement plan, and the $4,000 tax savings from your deduction is the same as in the previous examples: You reinvest those funds into an investment of some sort. For our examples, we've just been using a relatively conservative stock and bond portfolio.

We'll use the same portfolio return assumptions as our last two examples. At the end of the ten-year period, your $10,000 asset plus your $4,000 invested tax savings would be worth $23,090. That is a return of 130.90% over the ten-year period. As opposed to the first scenario, where you took a 60% loss the moment you spent the funds, in this scenario, you actually receive a 40% bonus the moment you invest your $10,000 retirement plan contribution.

CHOOSE YOUR DEDUCTIONS WISELY

Figure 3.1 shows what all three scenarios look like over our test period.

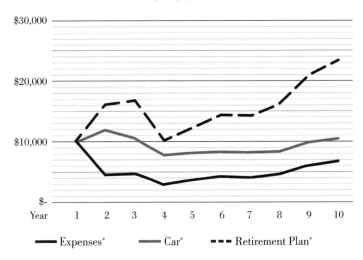

Follow the life of your deduction

Figure 3.1. *Based on S&P 500 index annual returns, 2005–2014. Please be aware you cannot invest directly in this index. Past performance is not indicative of future performance in any way.

Although no one can predict the markets and we certainly cannot rely on past performance to tell us what is going to happen in the future, it looks like the biggest bang for your tax deduction buck is in a retirement plan. You most certainly do not receive a meaningful benefit from your deduction by "creatively" inflating operational and office expenses, and definitely not by buying a company car.

COMBINING DEDUCTIONS

These deductions are gifts that keep on giving. When it comes to the operating expenses and the retirement plan, you can take these deductions every year. I increase these to more attractive and meaningful amounts and combine these, as (1) bona fide operating expenses for the development and operations of your business are appropriate and will always exist, and (2) if it is tax deductions you seek, I want to encourage you to use retirement plans as much as feasible and allowable. Business owners I work with are frequently surprised at just how large the deductions are when deploying retirement plans in their business. Let's look at a couple of scenarios and see what it might look like ten years down the road.

If we assume you will take the retirement and operating expense deductions every year for ten years and also assume you will buy a car every five years, what do we have to show for it at the end of the ten-year period?

The $100,000 invested in simply taking deductions for everything you can think of every year over the ten-year period amounts to $61,843 in reinvested taxes you saved, representing a −38.16% return on your cash flow versus a −100% return if you just spent the savings. The $20,000 invested in your two cars over the ten-year period results in a remaining value of $14,794 (the invested deductions plus the depreciated value of the cars, assuming you sold the cars for that amount at the end of each five-year period), representing a −26.03% return on your cash flow. The $100,000 invested in your retirement plan over the ten-year period results in $267,696 from the earnings on the account and the reinvested deductions, representing a 167.70% return on your cash flow.

Figure 3.2 represents the net cash flow invested for your future.

Follow the life of your deduction

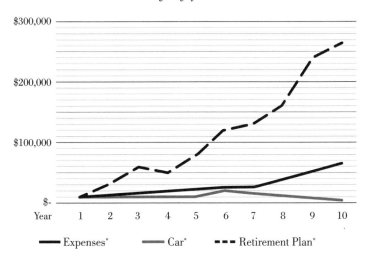

Figure 3.2. *Based on S&P 500 index annual returns, 2005–2014. Please be aware you cannot invest directly in this index. Past performance is not indicative of future performance in any way.*

My point here is to make decisions that are aligned with your long-term goals and of course your why. Think about what you want at the end of this endeavor of strategic tax planning and not just about the short-term gratification of the current year's deduction. If you are in a position to optimize and take advantage of all three, let's help you do that properly and prudently. If you are not in a position to deploy all three, you will want to look at your options at a level you are comfortable committing to for a few years.

It's not set in stone either. Discuss your planning on a regular basis with your expert team or when things measurably change in your life or your business. You can make changes to most plans; however, as said previously, some do require some commitment in years and amounts, so leave a cushion you are comfortable maintaining.

BEHAVIORAL FINANCE

It is important we pause for a moment to talk about behavioral finance. As we all know, money is not just about the dollars and cents. It most definitely is not about people always making rational decisions with the money. There is a whole field of work around the personalities we exhibit around our relationship with money. No matter what your type may be, those of us working to help you create and implement a plan need to remember there is a quantitative side of planning—what may technically make sense for someone. But the qualitative side of the equation may be of equal or sometimes even greater weight for some. Unfortunately, quite often money becomes an emotional issue, where decisions are made based on the present moment and not a long-term strategic decision as I'm advocating here. In my experience, the older we get, the better we are at this. Either way, these feelings are real and must be taken on board in order to develop a financial plan that lets them sleep at night.

Depression-era babies did a pretty good job of saving money, because they experienced the worst scenario possible when the market and economy crashed. Their parents drilled into them the importance of saving for their future, and they saw how hard living could get without a safety net. Baby boomers, Generation X babies, and now Millennials do not have this foundation. Let me put it this way: I've never had a seventy-year-old person in my office saying, "Gee, I wish I didn't save so much money my whole life."

People who save money throughout their working life have far more options and flexibility in making decisions about their business transition and their retirement plans than those who do not. It is that simple. It's important to remember this is your money, not the government's. Now, you decide which scenario you want for yourself, your family, and your legacy.

OPTIMIZE THIS OPPORTUNITY

How many people will take the $4,000 of tax savings and invest it? Data to answer this question does not seem to exist, but in my experience, it isn't a lot. Most people think of tax savings as bonus money rather than just part of their overall net income. A qualified retirement plan, especially some form of a defined benefit pension plan, will virtually force you to save. Many business owners are simply not aware of their options in this area. Even an independent professional with few or no employees has incredible options to consider when it comes to deploying employee benefit plans and retirement plans in their business. It's important to meet with a professional to see whether these plans are appropriate for your situation. Many of these plans require a consistent commitment to contributions for multiple years, requiring reliable cash flows in order to remain compliant.

Now, we have some clients at my firm who are incredibly successful at what they do. What I tell them is to do all of it. Let's take advantage of the tax code—and legally avoid tax—to benefit you and your business. However, if you're not in a situation with enough cash flow for all three strategies, you have to make strategic decisions of how you are using the situation and cash flow you have.

At a recent workshop I conducted with a room full of entrepreneurs ranging from startups to fully established ongoing concerns, I was asked if there is a limit on the amount of deductions you can take in your business. I was also asked if there is a level at which an IRS audit will be triggered. I actually let the CPA friend in the room answer this question to give some comfort to the group. Her answer was clear: There is not a limit, and there is not an IRS trigger. The deductions you choose to take must simply be substantiated as genuine business expenses.

There is one other major difference I am compelled to point out in the three scenarios just described: You cannot spend a car or a computer. Sure, you could sell the car and spend the proceeds, but that takes time and involves risk. Remember, it's a depreciating asset. Will you really be able to sell the car based on its condition for the full depreciated value? Given the rate at which technology advances, you are certainly not going to get a lot for your used computer.

The assets in the retirement account, however, are fully liquid to support your lifestyle during your retirement years. Of course, you need to be sure to wait until you are fifty-nine and a half years old (plans can be designed that allow deductions earlier) to avoid a penalty, and these assets are taxable at the time of withdrawal. It is most likely the compounding effect of the tax-deferred account is a far better use of your cash flow for tax deductions than any other.

There is a host of qualified retirement plans that have the potential to generate much larger deductions—and, therefore, savings—in a tax-deferred account. The savings in these plans have the potential to give you the largest deductions you can legally take, more than any deduction you could take for the purpose of simply avoiding the tax. Most qualified retirement plans do triple duty for you; that's how valuable they are. First, they give you large tax deductions. Next, they provide an excellent automatic savings and investment system. Finally, most plans provide for asset protection. I have developed plans for people that enabled hundreds of thousands of dollars in deductions.

Furthermore, if your spouse is a W-2 employee and you have a small business (or vice versa), there are very interesting options to help the deductions for the retirement plan in the small business offset the income from your spouse's W-2. This involves a careful design combining strategies in entity structuring with qualified employee benefit plans to create an overall greater benefit to the family as a whole rather than working in silos between spousal activities.

ASSET PROTECTION FROM LIABILITY AND CREDITORS

Wouldn't it be nice to have the ability to save large amounts of money for your retirement, receive a huge tax deduction for doing so, and have all of those funds you have saved protected from claimants? In most cases, the funds you save in a qualified retirement plan are not accessible to claims or judgments as a result of you getting sued or of a dispute with your debt holders.

This is not a minor feature. You should be aware that not only do you benefit in the present, by way of tax deductions, and in the long term, by way of savings, for this type of tax deduction, but it is actually a protection vehicle.

Just like any other decision in your business, the decisions about how to utilize your cash flow for legal tax deductions should be well thought out and strategic. You will want to think long term and have this strategy aligned with your goals and objectives as it relates to your growth, your protection from liability and creditors, and your transition plan.

Remember, it is not just about avoiding the big mistakes but also about learning how to take advantage of your unique opportunities. Tax planning is a significant opportunity available to successful entrepreneurs that isn't available to most other people in our society. If you fall into the trap of enhancing your deductions just for short-term gratification, you are letting the tax tail wag the whole dog.

Alternative plan options

A discussion about employee benefit plans would not be complete without including other options beyond the conventional qualified plans. There is another category of plans that may not bring you immediate deductions but will provide substantial benefits to you and your key employees in the future. Additionally, there are tools and techniques you may use independent of Department of Labor–approved plans.

So far, we have talked about qualified plans. Qualified

plans are those plans that are qualified for employee benefits and provide immediate tax deductions to the employer.
Most of these plans can legally be skewed within limits to
disproportionately benefit key employees and highly com-
pensated employees like you, the owner. There are other
plans referred to as nonqualified plans, which are permitted in certain types of entities. These generally benefit key
employees. These are things like nonqualified deferred
compensation funded with life insurance, group life insurance, and others.

There is a growing population of people who do not
want to invest capital in anything that will be taxable in
the future. For these healthy clients who can be under-
written, we illustrate the use of permanent life insurance,
which, if structured properly, has the ability to not just
provide a death benefit in the case of premature death
but provide tax-free income during their retirement. Yes,
while alive.

I cannot say which of these may or may not be the best
for you, but now you are armed with information to ask good
questions of your expert team.

ENTREPRENEURIAL ED

In looking at Ed's tax returns from the past several years,
we found he has been averaging around $200,000 in state
and federal income taxes annually. We then ran projections
forward for the next twenty years and were not surprised to

find he will be paying at least that every year going forward if he continues to structure and take income as he is today. How is it that Ed has an accounting professional and an estate attorney on his team and no one has suggested he change this structure? Answer: His tax person does not specialize in working with successful business owners, and Ed's attorney actually recommended he get a financial planner. But Ed's a smart guy and thought he was doing a good job as a do-it-yourselfer.

Ed and Edwina's entire tax strategy is to buy and deduct anything and everything they can. They push the limit on deductions with their real-estate business by traveling for "property searches" everywhere they love to travel. They purchase supplies, vehicles, technology, and more, far beyond anything necessary to run their business, with the single motivation to enhance deductions from their income every year. They're inappropriately using their business for their personal lifestyle enhancement.

They have not saved anything for retirement and have virtually no liquidity. Their wealth-building strategy for themselves and their family is accumulating properties. They face several challenges:

☐ They can't spend buildings. These properties are the legacy they intend to leave their children; however, they may need to sell some property to fund their retirement. Will their need to sell coincide with the right time to sell in the cycle of real estate and the greater macroeconomic environment?

☐ They have been overpaying taxes annually by
   approximately 40–50%.

☐ They have not sheltered any of their wealth or
   savings (in their case, property) from liability
   attack.

☐ Based on their goals and risk tolerance, it's
   too late to implement most of these strategies
   at this stage of their lives.

You may be shocked by that last one. Yes, it is too late.
Ed and Edwina are now in their late sixties and do not want
to continue to manage these properties as they have for
the past thirty years. Therefore, the tools and techniques
appropriate for someone in their current life stage are not
the same as those for someone in earlier life stages.

When I explained the situation, Ed's response was
"Why didn't my tax guy tell me about this years ago?"

SELF-ASSESSMENT

Are all of the deductions you take in your business needed for
growth and smooth operations? Create a second income statement stripping out all unnecessary expenses in order to produce
a pro forma income statement based on necessity.

How are you investing the net income of your firm today?

_____

Would you like to create or enhance your employee benefit programs? Would you still like to do so knowing not all of the benefit will go to you exclusively?_____

_____

What is the return on your deduction investment today?_____

_____

Bring the answers to these questions, along with your past three years of tax returns, to your financial planner for you to learn your options for investing your net income.

_____

Tax planning is a complex area of planning requiring longterm strategic thinking in order to develop a plan that is appropriate for your circumstance and aligned with your vision for your firm, your employees, you, and your family. Taking deductions just for the sake of deductions is not a long-term strategic plan. Clients who adopt such strategies are not being as efficient and effective with their tax flow as otherwise might be available to them. Many are just not educated on their options, along with the advantages and disadvantages of those options. Understanding those options makes you an informed executive to be empowered to make decisions you are comfortable making.

Think of your deductions as an expense for which you are using precious cash flow. Is that the highest and best use of that cash flow? Will it bear long-term benefit?

None of the tools and techniques I discuss in this book operate in their own silo. The careful interconnected design of all of these areas is crucial in order to have a plan that works for you toward your goals while staying compliant with the applicable authorities. There are opportunities to combine techniques in order to put your assets to work for you with even more benefit or protection.

Be sure to review your tax strategy on a regular basis or as your circumstances change.

Big Mistake #4

NOT PLANNING FOR WHAT COULD GO WRONG

"Living at risk is jumping off the cliff and
building your wings on the way down."
—Ray Bradbury

As I pointed out earlier, a true entrepreneurial spirit requires a special set of core characteristics in order to thrive and survive in both good times and bad. Among the most important of these characteristics is stick-to-itiveness. Yes, that's a word; look it up!

Stick-to-itiveness is a whole heck of a lot easier if you actually anticipate what can go wrong and then develop your strategy to deal with these setbacks as well as you can. It goes without saying: If you expect to achieve out-of-the-ordinary results, you have to take risks in business. However, just like the high-wire acrobat, we have to be prudent and play some defense as well. Of course, we cannot anticipate everything possible, but there are certain problems we can anticipate from history and experience.

Business continuity planning is this anticipation strategy harnessed to protect your company. To plan for continuity, you must analyze the possible threats and risks to your business that could impede your ability to deliver your product or service to the marketplace. Given the rapid rate of technology development and the general increase in threats from cyber or terrorist attacks, natural disasters, disease epidemics, technology failures, and civil unrest, business continuity planning has become a specialty profession. Consultants and coaches familiar with these threats are assets to your advisory team.

Using the US Census Bureau's "Business Dynamics Statistics" database, researcher Scott Shane plotted five-year survival rates by industry for firms founded in 2005 and published the results on America's Small Business Development Center's website (americassbdc.org). His analysis revealed that mortality rates for companies as an entity vary considerably by industry:

Industry	Five-year survival rate (%)
Mining	51.3
Manufacturing	48.4
Services	47.6
Wholesale	47.4
Agriculture	47.4
Retail	41.1
Finance/insurance/real estate	39.6
Transportation	39.4
Communications/utilities	39.4
Construction	36.4

Source: *Smallbiztrends.com*

As you can see, these numbers are not very impressive. The failure rate of businesses in the first five years is incredibly high. It is always difficult to run these studies in a vacuum, without including all sorts of outside factors in the statistics. In this case, the study started in boom time and went through one of the worst economic crashes since the Great Depression. Perhaps this has skewed these numbers toward the lower end of the spectrum, but we do know the five-year survival rate of startup businesses is historically not great.

Shane explained that 46% of the businesses failed due to "incompetence," including the following mistakes:

- ☐ An emotional approach to pricing

- ☐ No knowledge of industry pricing conventions

- ☐ Nonpayment of taxes

- ☐ No knowledge of financing requirements and conventions

- ☐ No experience in record-keeping

- ☐ Living beyond the means of the business

- ☐ Lack of planning

Most if not all of those areas are preventable with effective hiring and delegating, education, and changes in behavior. Other risks to a greater degree are out of your control and will require deployment of tools and techniques as part of an overall risk and asset protection plan.

Thirteen percent of the failures were due to fraud, natural disasters, and neglect. Armed with the knowledge there is a 13% chance of your company going out of business due to these factors makes it prudent to devote time and energy to evaluate your options to possibly cover some or all of those risks. Then you are in a position to understand the cost–benefit relationship to protect your business from those risks. At the end of that process, you may even decide you are willing to self-insure and absorb that risk and not do anything further to immunize your business from that particular risk.

What is the failure rate of more seasoned closely held businesses? It is difficult to find statistics on why businesses fail after they have been up and running for more than five or ten years. The information ranges from a lack of planning—again, poor transition planning—to only thinking about all the good happening and not the risks. This is not uncommon, but new entrepreneurs are more likely than most to be wearing rose-colored glasses, to be seduced by their success, and to ignore the risks just below the surface. This optimism is one of those critical characteristics of an entrepreneur, but it's a double-edged sword. You need to see both sides to keep your business afloat.

SWOT ANALYSIS

Most of you have probably heard of a SWOT analysis: strengths, weaknesses, opportunities, and threats.

Strengths and weaknesses are more about internal issues than external ones. Obviously, then, opportunities and threats are more about external issues than internal ones. The point of the exercise is a thorough analysis of what strengths and opportunities you can hone and exploit and what weaknesses and threats you can improve upon and protect against. These strengths and opportunities tend to be the market differentiators you can take advantage of, and you can take steps to protect them from loss or damage. They are your unique value adds you will want to highlight your intellectual property. You have most likely created barriers to entry for your potential competitors into your markets by using these elements to their fullest potential.

The analysis of weaknesses and threats tends to be focused on products, services, and processes, because, if left untended, they may hinder your ability to achieve your mission and vision. The external threats tend to include market trends and cycles, along with shortcomings in the business's products, services, and pricing vis-à-vis your competitors. The internal weaknesses include anything that puts you at a disadvantage to your competition—cost of operations, infrastructure, outdated equipment and technology, and perhaps weak links in human resources.

I have personally participated in numerous SWOT analyses during my career and have reviewed countless more in the process of preparing for this chapter. In my study and experience, I do not see enough focus on the internal weaknesses part of the exercise. Perhaps this is tinted by rose-colored glasses, but we tend to not spend enough time, effort, and financial resources to reduce and eliminate both weaknesses and threats.

When preparing for a SWOT analysis, I recommend you remove internal bias by hiring an outside party to come in and evaluate your situation independently from the majority owners and executive committee. This objective review will provide good, clean information for you to make decisions for changes or revisions to your current arrangements. Consider adding an advisory board made up of clients, mentors, and centers of influence in your network to provide input on their experience.

The feedback you receive from this process will unveil vulnerabilities you were aware of and some you were not. To the contrary, you may have unique advantages and opportunities you may not even know about. Quite often, we become immersed in our own world, unaware of changes outside our sphere that may open up new sources of revenue or technology innovation that may improve margins or quality of life in the work environment for your team.

Far too often, these exercises are ignored; do so at your own peril. It is an unfortunate situation when a company fails due to events that could have been avoided or whose impact could have been mitigated. It may sting even worse if ten or twenty years down the road, you realize significant opportunities were lost along the way that could have dramatically improved your success or reduced your vulnerabilities.

PEOPLE MAKE BUSINESSES SUCCESSFUL

Without great people to create, develop, produce, and deliver your product or service, the competitive marketplace will eat you for lunch. That's how capitalism works. We all need great people in our businesses to successfully compete. Without them, we do not stand a chance. When the economy is struggling, the pool of qualified employees and consultants is vast. However, when the economy is booming, the pool of qualified employees and consultants is sparse. Now consider the small percentage of talent that is the elite we all seek. These are the rock stars of your organization who make everything happen. Quite often, these people are not part of the available labor pool, even when the economy is doing poorly. The demand for the top talent we all want is always high, regardless of economic conditions. This type of talent, especially with a mutual fit for your organization, is a super-rare find.

This is especially important for small business owners, who need to think about what happens to the business if something happens to them or their elite talent. Smaller organizations suffer disproportionately to larger organizations when a key team member is temporarily or permanently absent. Have you seriously considered what happens to your business if something happens to any of your rock stars? Think about the bands and singing groups you've known throughout your lifetime. The list of groups forced to disband when the lead is sick, quits, or dies is going to be very long. In small businesses, these questions are normally focused on the owner, but it is also important to think about these questions as they relate to your key employees. Whether your business is large or small, there may be key team members who are critical to you achieving your mission and vision. If they go down, even temporarily, what will the ramifications be at each and every stage of your supply chain to deliver your product or service on time with the same high level of quality?

Maybe you are the rock star in your business. What happens to your business if something happens to you? What if you become sick or injured? What happens if you or your business partner becomes ill, is injured, or dies unexpectedly? Professional service organizations, such as attorneys, tax professionals, health-care professionals, real-estate professionals, and so on, are particularly susceptible to their businesses struggling without their expertise, knowledge, and connections. For example, I have several physician clients. If something—heaven forbid—happens to them, and they don't have the right continuity plan in place, their business is going to fail— and quickly.

Can the business withstand the loss? What strategies do you have in place today to help you withstand the loss? What strategies do you need to add or change to help the firm withstand the loss?

Before reading on, please take a moment to seriously consider those questions.

HAVE A GOOD DEFENSE

Once your firm achieves a stable level of growth and profit, it has likely reached a point when the prudent entrepreneur will want to not just consider playing offense but also think about playing some defense. As entrepreneurs, it's common for us to think about playing offense, especially in the early years, when we are focused on brand awareness and growth. But just as any championship team you can think of in sports, you must develop your defensive game in business for your long-term game plan. If we are striving for long-term sustainability and growth, we have to excel at both types of play.

I know it's not fun to think about the bad things that can happen; of course, most of us want to be positive and optimistic. But we have to also be realistic. I like to use the following metaphor, which I alluded to earlier: Life is not a slow paddle across a flat, calm lake. It's more like a whitewater river-rafting trip with unexpected twists, turns, and the occasional hidden boulder that suddenly pops up in the middle of our world. Most of the time, this boulder appears at the worst possible moment—just as we think we are going to float by, enjoying the view.

Oh, that will never happen to me, you might be thinking. Sure, we hear about all sorts of horrible family events, illnesses, and injuries that happen to people we know, but we can't imagine it ever happening to us.

Consider these facts: Most working Americans estimate that their own chances of experiencing a long-term disability are substantially lower than the average worker's.[2] Sixty-four percent of wage earners believe they have a 2% or less chance of being disabled for three months or longer during their working career; the actual odds of this happening to a worker entering the workforce today are about one in four: 25%.[3]

ARE YOU INSURED FOR DISABILITY FOR YOURSELF OR YOUR KEY EMPLOYEES?

I bet you're insured for the following unfortunate events. Let's compare the odds.

☐ Chances your household will have a reported home fire: 25%[4]

☐ Drivers file a claim for a collision, on average, once every 17.9 years[5]

☐ Chances of a major (magnitude 7.5 or higher)

---

2 Council for Disability Awareness, "CDA 2010 Council for Disability Awareness Survey: The Disability Divide," http://www. disabilitycanhappen.org/research/consumer

3 US Social Security Administration, Fact Sheet, February 7, 2013, https://www.ssa.gov/disabilityfacts/facts.html

4 National Fire Protection Association, http://www.nfpa.org/news-and -research/fire-statistics-and-reports/fire-statistics/fires-by-property-type/ residential/a-few-facts-at-the-household-level

5 *Forbes*, http://www.forbes.com/sites/moneybuilder/2011/07/27/how-many -times-will-you-crash-your-car/#44b8148f50f9

earthquake in California in the next thirty years: 46%; chances of magnitude 6.7 or higher: 99%[6]

I could go on and on with statistics, but suffice it to say, premature or unexpected death and disability happens more frequently than we are willing to admit. It can happen to you.

I don't know about you, but in the past several years I have lost several friends who have passed away suddenly in their fifties. The various reasons for their tragic deaths at such an early age range from heart attacks and cancer to horrible accidents. They were taken from us way too young. Their families and their friends have suffered terribly from these early losses, and it just breaks my heart to think of it. Some of them were prepared and left their family in a good place to do their best to pick up the pieces and move on with their own lives. Some were not and the family has to not only grieve the loss of the loved one but figure out how they are going to support themselves going forward.

Another consideration I want to encourage you to evaluate also leads into the transition plan for the business. If a catastrophic event affects one of the principals in the business, there should be a clear method of business transition

---

6 "For northern California, the most likely source of such earthquakes is the Hayward-Rodgers Creek Fault (31% in the next 30 years). Such quakes can be deadly, as shown by the 1989 magnitude 6.9 Loma Prieta and the 1994 magnitude 6.7 Northridge earthquakes." usgs.gov

to the other principals, if any, or to other appropriate heirs. It is important for the business to continue to operate and to maintain its value during any transition process; the tragic death of an owner is no different. Planning to mitigate any disruption in the business is in the best interests of all parties involved.

WHAT TO DO ABOUT IT?

Request that your planning quarterback professional illustrate these asymmetrical events in your plan. I call this "stress testing" the plan. The exercise should simulate the impact of these events on short-term cash flow and the longer-term vision you have for building and protecting your wealth. If a need, gap, or risk is identified, the next step is to illustrate your options to deploy tools and techniques that could mitigate the risks and narrow the gaps.

In addition to creating a general business continuity plan for natural disasters, power outages, and terrorist attacks, you will want to evaluate the impact of a key employee loss, both temporary and permanent. Everyone's situation is different. These suggestions should not be taken as specific recommendations, but the basic principles can empower you to ask good questions and make informed decisions.

Here are some options to consider:

Buy–sell agreements

Buy–sell agreements need to be very detailed and to include the method for determining value for triggering events. What is the source of capital to allow the surviving partner to execute their requirements in the agreement? What is the payment schedule? Are there any contingencies to protect the surviving partner and the spouse?

Individual disability insurance

Individual disability insurance may be a suitable tool to provide a source of capital to help your family should you become disabled and unable to earn your normal income. Long-term disability is normally for those who cannot perform the regular duties of their work for over ninety or 180 days (the *elimination period*), depending on the type of policy. The shorter the elimination period, the higher the premium will most likely be.

Business overhead insurance

Business overhead insurance may be a suitable tool to provide a source of capital to help the owner cover operating expenses and temporary replacement staff should the insured become disabled and not able to perform their normal duties long term. This is a very important tool for independent professionals when they are most likely the key employee. Think about how nice it would be to have the ability to hire someone to take care of your customers, clients, and patients and keep things going while you recover.

Company- or partnership-owned disability insurance

Company- or partnership-owned disability insurance may be a suitable tool to provide a source of capital to help the owner cover operating expenses and temporary replacement staff should the insured become disabled and not able to perform their normal duties.

Company- or partnership-owned life insurance

Company- or partnership-owned life insurance may be a suitable tool to provide a source of capital to help the surviving owner buy out the heirs of a deceased owner per the buy–sell agreement in place. Most buy–sell agreements are funded with life insurance.

Key man disability insurance

Key man disability insurance is purchased by the owner on the life of the key employee. Should this employee become disabled, this insurance will provide capital to temporarily replace the employee or hire an outside contractor or firm to support the company and make up the void of missing this important member of the team.

Key man life insurance

Key man life insurance is purchased by the company on the life of the key employee in order to provide important funding to replace this critical team member. This may not cover everything, but key man insurance is there to provide this much-needed capital, to keep operations running smoothly, and to maintain the client base.

You will want to become educated on your options for tools and techniques, along with the advantages and disadvantages for each. This includes the decision to act only in a limited fashion or to do nothing at all. Once you have this fully evaluated, you can understand the costs to then determine the cost-to-benefit relationship so you make sound decisions.

Is the most important asset in your business you or other people? Protect yourself and your business from the loss of important assets.

ENTREPRENEURIAL ED

For the past twenty years, Ed has been running the real-estate business with virtually no backup plan. If something were to happen to Ed, his business would be disrupted, but he's fortunate his revenue would not.

Ed operates everything himself and has not written anything down for others to be able to help or take over if he should be incapacitated. He may have problems with bills getting paid, and his wife and children may have a very frustrating several months of picking up the mess, but the rents would keep coming in, and they would be taken care of quite well.

Ed would be wise to write everything down and to train his son or daughter on how he operates his buildings, maintenance and upkeep schedules, and the finances of his real-estate business. He has been pretty lucky at finding tenants when vacancies arise but has not shared his process with anyone in the family.

Unfortunately, the same cannot be said if Ed should suddenly die. For example, when applying very conservative growth rates on Ed's real-estate fortune, his family is estimated to have an estate tax liquidity deficit as follows:

☐ If Ed dies now: $4,200,000 cash deficit

☐ If Ed dies in five years: $5,100,000 cash deficit

☐ If Ed dies at age ninety: $9,400,000 cash deficit

When an estate has a liquidity deficit, the heirs are forced to sell assets in order to pay the Internal Revenue Service the tax due within nine months of someone's death. In Ed's situation, should Edwina outlive him, Edwina will find severe disruption in income and net worth due to this forced sale of several of the properties to pay the tax. Based on their current arrangements, the estate tax alone Edwina would pay upon Ed's death is approximately $3.8 million.

Other clients are not in such a fortunate situation. Over the years my client list of successful entrepreneurs has spanned the range of industries and professions that are vulnerable to this type of disruption. I'll describe just one.

A physician client has a unique practice and is an outlier in the level of revenue he produces for a general practitioner. His gross income is five times the average annual income for someone in his field. Patients come to him in droves; because he has served a captive market for decades, he provides a unique service, and people like him. If something should happen to him, there is no business.

He has been known to put off his own needed healthcare treatments because the recovery and recuperation period would cost him thousands of dollars in the days he would not be able to see his own patients. Just imagine if he had a long-term disability causing him to miss six to twelve months of work.

SELF-ASSESSMENT

Let's try a basic self-exam. Sit back and think about the following questions seriously, then write down your answers. Don't just think about these scenarios in the abstract; get concrete. We take things much more seriously and then have a much higher likelihood of taking action if we write it down.

What will happen to your business and family if you become disabled for more than ninety days?_____

_____

What will happen to your business and family if you die suddenly and unexpectedly?_____

_____

How many clients, customers, and patients will you lose if you, your partner, or any key employee cannot perform their responsibilities in the delivery of your product or service? _____

How quickly will this loss occur? _____

What is the loss of revenue over three, six, nine, twelve, and twenty-four months?_____

_____

Will clients, customers, and patients come back when you do? Be realistic!_____

_____

What is the source of capital to help pay your overhead expenses while you are out and have reduced income? _____

_____

Will you be able to bring in a temporary replacement? What will that cost be? What is the source of capital to pay this person?

_____

What will happen to your business if you are forced to retire due to medical reasons?_____

_____

Will your business partner's spouse or other heirs be your new partner if your current partner dies unexpectedly? _____

_____

What is the source of capital for your spouse or other heirs to be paid for the value of your share of the business if you die unexpectedly? What is the formula for that value to be determined? _____

_____

What is the source of capital for your spouse or other heirs to pay estate taxes if you die unexpectedly? What is the formula for that value to be determined? _____

_____

_____

Now that you've covered the basics to evaluate whether you have a need or concern, the next step is to take action by meeting with a specialist who can help you.

Business continuity planning doesn't need to be confined to planning for natural disasters and terrorism. All businesses rely on the people to achieve their mission and vision. Successful entrepreneurs will want to evaluate the impact that losing a mission-critical team member for a short or long period of time will have on the revenue, expenses, client retention, and sustainability of their firm.

However optimistic we want to be in our general spirit, any thorough planning process should include not only what your plans for growth and prosperity may be—that is, playing offense—but also what your plans are to protect your business from potential life events that may act like the proverbial boulder in your whitewater-rafting trip—that is, playing defense. How will things fare when something doesn't go according to plan? Putting appropriate tools in place to avoid or mitigate a potentially catastrophic event is having your wings in place so you can feel free to take that leap from the cliff.

Big Mistake #5

INADEQUATE
PROTECTION FROM
WEALTH PREDATORS

"It's not what you make; it's what you keep that counts."
—reportedly, Warren Buffett

Logically, we all know it's what you keep that counts. Of course, top-line health and growth is important, but it doesn't matter if it is squandered or placed at undue or unnecessary risk of decay or loss. We all also know far more wealth has been lost over history than kept. There are five major wealth predators in our society that undermine our ability to keep wealth. These are the common things that cause our hard-earned, hard-saved wealth to be eroded or even completely destroyed.

Let's start by looking at one of the most famous buildings in the world. The Pentagon is the largest office building in the world. It was designed in 1941 by architect George

Bergstrom and was built in record time to consolidate all the fast-growing defense and national security personnel for the World War II effort. Before it was built, there were approximately 24,000 members of the War Department in seventeen buildings spread throughout Washington, DC, and Virginia. The generals expected to need to accommodate over 40,000 people and wanted it to be ready within six months. Even while it was being built, the Defense Department was growing faster than expected, and they had to add two floors to the plans. At one time, there were close to 13,000 workers on the site, building at a frenetic pace.

This important building would house some of the most critical people for planning and executing World War II, in which over 12 million people served from 1938 to 1945. At the risk of stating the obvious, the safety and security of this building and the people working in it is crucial, twenty-four hours a day. Despite the risk of having the entire War Department, including its most senior members, in one building, Secretary of War Henry L. Stimson informed President Roosevelt that the department would see a 25–40% improvement in efficiency if they were under one roof.

The building is shaped, of course, like a pentagon. Truth be told, the pentagonal outer shape was derived out of necessity; the shape of the land they chose dictated it. After a weekend of arguing, the designers settled on this shape as the best option to have the highest efficiency, the best use of the land, and a visually appealing architecture design.

The offices are organized into five concentric rings

around a center courtyard. Each ring is further divided into sections, called wedges. Each wedge is designed to be reinforced and to contain any damage within it, so that the next wedge is safe from any attack or damage. Within the wedges, the concentric rings allow the inner layers to be more secure. The wedge that bore the brunt of the terrorist attack on 9/11 is called Wedge 1; they were named clockwise from the tip of the pentagon shape. Wedge 1 had just recently been renovated and reinforced to modernize the design for today's threats. Eighty percent of the people who work in Wedge 1 had returned to their offices after the renovation and were there when the Boeing 757 struck the building; 20,000 people were inside the building, with approximately 2,800 people inside Wedge 1 at the time of the attack. Although it is still a tragic, horrible event, only 125 Pentagon employees were killed. The design and reinforcement work has been hailed as a key reason more people did not die on that fateful day.

The design concept of layers of protection combined with sectional reinforcement is an image I'd like you to keep in mind as we walk through the five wealth predators.

WEALTH PREDATOR 1: TAXES

Taxes are one of those predators that keep coming back around, year after year after year. They're like a piece of gum you stepped in weeks ago; no matter how much you scrape your shoe, it just won't go away. There are many taxes we pay throughout the course of the day, some of which we hardly even notice. Some of them are hidden in your restaurant bill, your gas bill, your power bill, your wine bill, and so on. These are taxes we have very little control over paying. However, the biggest and most common of the taxes are things we do have some control over—actually more than you think. These, of course, are income taxes—federal and state income taxes, capital gains tax, and estate tax.

So why do I call the tax system a predator? When you combine all of the taxes we pay, especially in states with a state income tax, more than 50% of the income of high-income taxpayers goes to various government entities.[7] These are the same government entities run by both political parties that have a very solid and the most consistently reliable historical pattern in the history of the world of being horrible stewards of our money.

It is also true that you have the unalienable right to overpay your taxes. Consider that, in 2013, the top 10% of taxpayers paid 71% of the federal taxes. I have met people who don't want to even do the basics of tax planning, for fear they will be audited one day. To paraphrase a quote attributed to Judge Learned Hand, it is completely within one's rights to arrange their affairs in order to minimize their tax liability to the government. This is the difference

---

7 https://www.ftb.ca.gov/forms/2016-California-Tax-Rates-and-Exemptions .shtml, https://www.irs.gov/publications/p17/ar02.html

between tax evasion (illegal) and tax avoidance (legal). The former gets you a long prison sentence, and the latter allows you to decide the most efficient and best use of your hard-earned, hard-saved capital.

If you start early enough, successful small- to mid-sized business owners like you have the potential to substantially, if not completely, save for retirement just by doing proper tax planning throughout your peak earning years. The money you save on the taxes alone has the ability to virtually fund your basic retirement needs. I repeat this purposely to remind you and get your attention on how important this element is in your financial planning. Quite frequently, I review tax returns of prospective clients only to find they have been paying unnecessarily high income taxes. These people are often paying six and seven figures in taxes and have been doing so for years.

It isn't possible in every situation, but I have helped clients cut these taxes dramatically. Think about how much you save over ten years, over twenty years, or more. Now apply a growth rate to those savings, just like we did earlier; pick something conservative. Now apply the compounding effect of savings and growth over that twenty-year period. If the savings is in a tax-qualified account, we need to analyze this mountain of savings as tax-deferred growth as well. That builds a substantial nest egg.

But that's not the only benefit to the tax-qualified savings strategy; we get a double benefit there. Remember, it is highly likely the funds you save into a tax-qualified plan will have protection from exposure to liability and creditors (which is wealth predator 2 below).

Capital gains taxes are another tax eroding wealth. I find most people think long-term capital gains tax rates are 15%. However, at the highest level, capital gains taxes are 20%. This tax surprises a lot of people when they go to sell their business or real-estate investors when they sell a property. The surprise comes when these clients realize they will have to pay state income taxes and the Medicare supplemental tax created as part of the Affordable Care Act (Obamacare) of 3.8% on top of it. That's not all. If depreciation was taken on any of the assets being sold, that depreciation will have to be recaptured, up to a rate of 25%. For example, in California, people are shocked to learn that when the sales windfall will be added to their income for that year, they will have to pay over 40% in capital gains taxes. That's a whole lot more than 15%.

The most onerous of taxes in our society is the estate tax. When someone dies, their estate is valued, and if they are over the exclusion amount, they have to pay a huge assessment for being successful. We are not talking about a small penalty for success. Estate tax rates have had wide ranges over the years. Currently, the top rate impacts single payers at a rate of 40%, with a taxable estate over $5.5 million, couples over $11 million. These are very high amounts, but clients who own property in highly metropolitan areas and who own businesses are finding it easier to reach these levels than one might think. Also often forgotten is adding personally owned life insurance to the calculation. Mind you, this is income and assets that have already been taxed. There is no other way to describe it than a redistribution of wealth, with the political class deciding what to do with your hard-earned success.

Taxes are the biggest of all the wealth predators in our society warranting time and attention by you and your expert team of advisors.

WEALTH PREDATOR 2: LITIGATION

When you achieve a measure of success, you become an attractive target for someone to sue for even the most harmless claims. As we all know, there are people who abuse and manipulate our civil code to extract wealth from the producers of our society and give it to relative nonproducers of our society, including themselves. Many defendants know it is not worth the trouble to fight the lawsuit and simply settle out of court.

How bad is it?

The Court Statistics Project (CSP)—a joint project of the National Center for State Courts (NCSC) and the Conference of State Court Administrators (COSCA)—publishes caseload data from the courts of the fifty states, the District of Columbia, and Puerto Rico on their website, courtstatistics.org. According to their statistics, in 2015, with five states, including massive California, still unreported, there were just under 14 million civil lawsuits filed in the United States. That's the equivalent of

☐ 38,356 lawsuits per day

☐ 1,598 lawsuits per hour

☐ 26 ½ lawsuits per minute

This sue-happy culture is costly not just for the company or business owner being sued but for the rest of the country as well. Have a look at the table for some concrete numbers. Texas came in with the most number of cases, at just under 849,000, but Maryland actually wins by a landslide when it comes to the number of cases based on population, 15,230 cases per thousand residents per year. Perhaps being close to Washington, DC, has something to do with that. A strong case for tort reform in the United States. Suffice it to say, we live in a very litigious society.

Annual cost to the US economy for civil lawsuits	$239,000,000,000
Estimated annual cost to each US citizen for civil lawsuits	$812
Percentage of people who believe advertising by personal-injury lawyers encourages people to sue, even if they have not been injured	79%
Average compensation payout for injury lawsuits	$60,000
Percentage of punitive damages suits won by plaintiff	6%
Average awarded in a punitive damage lawsuit	$50,000

Source: statisticbrain.com

Now, it must be said there are civil courts for a reason. Bad actors hurt good people. The good people must have a process and system to support recompense from the bad actors if, and that's a big if, plaintiffs can prove their case. In the worst of all incidents, punitive damages are also warranted. If our system included the recovery of defendant costs when they are found not to be liable, we would reduce the flood of frivolous lawsuits to a trickle. The lobbying efforts against such reform are massive and will be fought vigorously.

Why should you care?

I find those numbers absolutely outrageous. I don't just view this as a predator of the personal wealth of those who get sued, but I also view frivolous lawsuit plaintiffs—and their legal counsel—as predators of the US macroeconomic environment in general. They take from overall GDP growth potential in the loss of growth and jobs. Just think about the amount of resources in the form of human capital, time, effort, energy, and money that goes to this process. Those resources would be far better deployed by getting to work building, growing, employing people, and creating productivity—ultimately growing wealth for many. Unfortunately, business owners—the people who create that growth and employment—are especially susceptible to lawsuits.

An article by SixWise[8] claimed, "Frivolous lawsuits

---

8 SixWise, "How Many Lawsuits are There in the U.S. & What are They For? An Amazing Overview," SixWise website, http://www.sixwise.com/ newsletters/06/10/05/how-many-lawsuits-are-there-in-the-us--amp-what -are-they-for-an-amazing-overview.htm

alone are said to cost the United States $200 billion a year, according to Congressman Terry Everett, and all of these potentially unwarranted claims are having an effect on how Americans view the legal system. According to a survey conducted by Harris Interactive, 76% of those surveyed feel that fear of frivolous lawsuits discourages people from performing normal activities."

Certain professions and activities are particularly vulnerable, including most in medicine, construction, architecture, real estate, manufacturing, and so on. If you employ people, you are subject to all sorts of common suits, such as workplace injuries, discrimination, harassment, and wrongful termination.

This area of risk—arguably, growing risk—warrants even more scrutiny from you and your advisors when developing your strategic business and personal plans such that you have an integrated plan that includes estate planning. It is prudent for you to avoid unnecessary exposure to this predator to your time, energy, opportunities, reputation, and wealth.

WHAT TO DO ABOUT IT

Much like the Pentagon, we want to place the assets we care about protecting as close to the center of our integrated financial plan as possible. From there, we want to section off or isolate some assets from making other assets vulnerable due to *their* unique and particular exposure to risk of loss or lawsuits. Now we can build a series of layers of protection using tools and techniques—shields—available for planners, depending on your particular situation. This multilayer approach cannot fully eliminate all exposure to liability, but it can greatly reduce your exposure and limit the damage a vengeful acquaintance may be able to create. The leech may be able to penetrate a layer of skin, but they won't be able to bleed you dry.

The first layer most people think of is insurance. A good general umbrella policy is prudent for basic situations. Once you start to incorporate more assets into your life, the umbrella policy will need to be larger and larger. Liability insurance is generally inexpensive if you do not have special risk exposures, which would cause premiums to rise. Other insurance products that may be required depending on your profession should be deployed, including errors and omissions insurance, and so on.

The common mistake we see with insurance is a lack of review of coverages to be sure they remain aligned with your level of wealth and your exposure to additional risks after the insurance is originally put in place. The other mistake we find is a complete reliance on insurance as the client's only shield of protection, a complacent strategy that may fail to protect them from even larger liability exposure.

The second layer commonly used to constrict open corridors to liability and creditors is entity structuring. Remember, we talked about how proper entity structuring can help provide multiple benefits to your comprehensive wealth and estate planning? As it relates to our Pentagon metaphor, entity structuring is a way to section off assets from creating vulnerability—and, therefore, exposure to liability from your other assets and liabilities, such as a building or the business itself. If you get sued, the predator can go after the assets inside that entity, but they're not likely going to be able to get to things outside that entity.

Be sure to properly consult with your expert team of advisors to be sure you are setting things up correctly and that you stay compliant. The common mistake here is comingling of finances, employees, clients, and so on between entities. It is important that each entity is a bona fide business and maintains its own books and records.

The third layer is a technique that could represent multiple shields, depending on the situation. This is the clever use of a combination of qualified and nonqualified, fringe-benefit, executive-benefit, retirement, insurance, and deferred-compensation plans. Again, purposely repeating myself here to be sure I send this message, most people do not realize the assets inside many of these plans are not available to liability and creditors. There are many examples of this in the public domain, where this strategy has worked quite effectively to protect assets from and for bad actors in our society. By the way, the finance industry uses some funny language that sometimes makes things sound like they are illegal. Nonqualified plans are perfectly legal and are more distinguished by their tax treatment not being qualified for a current tax deduction rather than the perception they are not permitted. Don't forget about tax planning and not letting the tax tail wag the dog. Choose your deductions wisely. How are you using your cash flow? Using your cash flow to not only protect it for your retirement but concurrently protect it from exposure to the predators of our society is a dual benefit from a single tactic in your overall tax and asset protection strategies.

Charitable trusts as part of your estate planning also have a dual benefit. They can potentially help great causes you care about deeply while also providing you, the donor, with lifetime income, current tax benefits, estate tax reduction or elimination, and protection from liability and creditors.

Your tax planning strategy may integrate any or all of these strategies. The field of protecting people from litigation is an art form, and there are many tools and techniques available to your expert team of advisors to deploy individually or in the right combination in order to address your unique circumstances.

The common mistake we see in this area in general are the extremes: Either we see people do nothing whatsoever, or we see people with incredibly complex structuring that makes it difficult to understand and very expensive to maintain. There's a happy medium in there somewhere; you just have to find yours.

WEALTH PREDATOR 3: THE BIG D—DIVORCE

The statistics about the divorce rate in the United States vary widely, depending on a lot of factors. Many reports say the divorce rate has now hit 50%. Yes, that's 5–0. But among the many elements this number depends on is what decade you were born or married, whether you had children or waited till a later age, and whether or not you lived together prior to getting married. Many of these factors are just common sense, as society's mores have changed over the years, and there are far more women in the workplace than there were several decades ago. Additionally, couples divorce less frequently or later in life if the couple has children versus those who do not.

Some interesting statistics: According to the Survey of Income and Program Participation, which can be found on the Centers for Disease Control website,[9] the rates of divorce have actually gone down in the past several decades. If you were married in the 1960s the divorce rate is just under 40%, the 1970s just over 45%, and if you were married in the 1980s, your divorce rate is close to 50%. However, there has been a steady decline since then. If you were married in the 1990s, your divorce rate is just under 35%, and in the 2000s, which is obviously still playing out, the divorce rate for those couples is around

---

9 https://www.cdc.gov/nchs/nvss/marriage-divorce.htm

15%. However you look at it, divorce rates are devastating to families and their wealth.

People ask me why divorce is a wealth predator. Let's start with a small example to illustrate a point, and then we can easily extrapolate that into a larger context. Imagine we have a couple who decides to start implementing their estate plan, which incorporates regular gifting to their children and grandchildren. Each of their three adult children will receive the annual gifts up to the current annual gift exclusion level from both Mom and Dad. At the time I write this to you, that equals $14,000 per person. That would then obviously mean each child is going to receive $28,000 annually from their parents.

Gifts are gifts, which means once the parents make the gift, it is an unconditional gift. This means the parents cannot dictate what happens to those funds once they are transferred from one account to the other. This giving up of control while watching children spend money in a manner that is not acceptable to the gifting parent or grandparent is very difficult for many.

As soon as the children deposit those funds into an account that has any marital assets combined with their spouse, those funds themselves will now be considered marital assets of that young couple. In just ten years of gifting, with an annual rate of return of 6%, the value of those funds would theoretically be $419,206. What will happen if, after ten years, this couple tragically ends their marriage in divorce? Most likely, half of the $419,206 is going to go to the now-ex-daughter- or son-in-law. How do you think the parents feel about the gifting now? Multiply this down to grandchildren. Ouch!

Remember, this is a basic example with minimal gifting. When implementing advanced estate plans, the tools and techniques deployed could transfer significantly greater amounts than this. Additionally, business transfers and other strategies may be executed in order to transfer wealth to future generations to legally avoid estate taxes in the current generation.

This becomes a very delicate area in the law and in family meetings. We are not here to dispense legal advice, but you can imagine the complications that come into play during divorce proceedings involving complex estates. The next Thanksgiving dinner may be a tragedy if someone in the family goes through a divorce, causing significant family wealth to walk away as a result of their failed love.

WHAT CAN BE DONE TO MITIGATE THIS RISK?

It is possible to alleviate much of the risk; however, many of the solutions challenge the relationships between parents and children, between spouses, and among the siblings themselves.

The first level of protection from this issue is a prenuptial agreement. If there is significant family wealth, I am a very strong proponent of prenuptial agreements.

An agreement properly structured by the attorney on your expert team in collaboration with your financial advisor will enable them to conduct a family meeting to educate everyone as to why this makes sense for the family. Prenuptial agreements are there to protect everyone, even the spouse coming to the marriage without significant wealth.

Additionally, depending on the state you live in, you or your expert should identify how community-property and divorce laws will dictate the need for more advanced planning. Family foundations and limited partnerships can be created to protect more wealth, but in the end, you have to hope your children and grandchildren make good decisions.

The common mistake here is people holding back on actually doing their wealth and estate planning. If they have gone through the planning process and have still not implemented the plan that involved gifting or giving up control of significant assets, they may be delaying in fear of the decisions their children are making. Their financial plan has become a dust-collecting fixture on the shelf in the home office, where it can do no one any good. Remember, wealth is everything we gain in life that death cannot take away. We cannot control everything, especially once we leave this universe. Divorce, number three.

WEALTH PREDATOR 4: BAD DECISIONS OR—EVEN WORSE— NO DECISIONS

Everyone has their own process for making decisions. Some people want all of the details, and some only want high-level features, risks, costs, and benefits. It doesn't matter to me what your process or style is for making decisions, as long as that process leads you to an informed decision in a reasonable time frame. Once you determine the options for achieving your vision and protecting yourself along the way—along with the advantages, disadvantages, risks, fees, and exit options for doing so—you'll be a long way toward being ready to make a decision.

Some decision-makers continuously seek more and more information—more details, more scenarios, more what-ifs. This can stifle your ability to actually make the decision. You may not have found the best approach to understanding the details, or you may not have found the right expert to explain it.

Some people just won't ever be comfortable enough to make a decision—even the decision to say no. None of us wants to disappoint others, and sometimes we hedge or delay to avoid rejecting a proposed action plan. It's easier for everyone if you just say no. Sometimes we are just frozen. The issue is so far out of our comfort zone we are just stuck on the proverbial glacier. I call this the procrastination glacier. Not making a decision is also a decision, and it can have just as damaging effects as choosing the wrong option. Don't forget, while you are prolonging your final decisions, time keeps on ticking and your competition is moving forward.

When we are making major decisions, there is no guarantee of the outcome. This can be discomforting. This is why I recommend you develop a process for making important decisions. If you've done well at implementing the first two chapters of the book, now is a good time to rely heavily on your team of trusted advisors. Do you need to invite in a specialist for this particular decision? As a team, they should be collaborating to understand your perspective and the options or proposals in front of you. Their counsel will guide you through, so you can be comfortable to make a decision in your best interest in the least amount of time necessary. Sorry to keep bringing you back here, but remember your why. This is the reason you did the hard work early in the book to keep you centered and remove all the flak flying around in your head and your life. Sit back for a couple of minutes and imagine your long-range personal and business vision, and determine which decision will lead you there.

WEALTH PREDATOR 5: THE CONVENTIONAL "WISDOM" OF WALL STREET

The conventional "wisdom" of Wall Street overwhelmingly dictates a singular investment philosophy that may not be suitable for all investors. Even though the concept was part of a PhD dissertation way back in 1952, it is actually called *"modern" portfolio theory* (MPT). In its simplest form, MPT wisely encourages us to create diversified portfolios divided between equities and fixed income and rebalance back to our original allocation on a regular basis—usually quarterly. This original asset allocation should reflect the investor's investment objective, risk tolerance, and time horizon to use the funds. It also promotes staying fully invested in the markets at all times. Cash is not meant to be part of the portfolio, except to allow enough to pay advisor and account fees and expenses. Of course we'll all create a system where we get paid.

The first part of it sounds fine and makes complete sense. We want diversified portfolios so you are not taking unnecessary risk in any one asset or asset class. For some, the rest of it is where MPT is not so modern. In fully using MPT, the money manager would not take into account anything that may be trending in the current cycle of the economy, including interest rates, recessions, or changes in any particular industry or sector. Meaning the manager would not seek to actively take advantage of those trends, nor would they seek to protect the investor from any negative trends in any major asset class. For this reason, many actually describe it as "buy, hold, and hope."

MPT has also made it too easy for many advisors. Many advisors have lost the fact that this is about people, not about just conforming to compliance departments and computer programs. The field has lost its personal connection to clients and has become more plug-and-play, based on a sterile set of questions that results in placing the client in one of five boxes. These boxes determine your investment objective and thus your supposed risk tolerance. From there you are placed into a plug-and-play investment strategy and the advisor is done. The computers take it from there, and regardless of anything happening in the world, your account will be automatically rebalanced back to the original allocation each January, April, July, and October, or however that advisor sets it, along with everyone else.

Technically there is nothing wrong with that philosophy. Full disclosure—my firm offers this classic form of investing, which we refer to as strategic asset management, for those who prefer this investment style. However, we also offer dynamic asset management for those who would like their investments to strive to not just grow the assets but protect them as well.

As I will illustrate in greater detail with a personal story in the next chapter, the advisor community would better serve their clients by fully understanding them and offer investment solutions and processes that fit the client sitting in front of them. I find the lack of options for people particularly troubling given we continually have bubble–burst cycles in our economy and thus cause major swings in our markets.

As you can see, I have put quotation marks around the word modern; I find it difficult to use that word to discuss a theory introduced more than sixty years ago, at the middle of the previous century. I don't know about you, but I think a few things have changed a bit since 1952 that might cause MPT to be more ancient than modern.

Of course, the Internet didn't exist in 1952. No one would have thought that the average investor with a few thousand dollars could self-direct their own account. Even more, none of us would have thought they would have access to the vast depth and breadth of information freely available at the tip of their fingers. We laugh now at the www before Internet addresses, but it actually means something—World Wide Web. So now people all over the world, regardless of their level of education, may have access to information that would allow them to do research to invest their own savings. This has dramatically increased the number of participants creating demand in the investment markets.

The adoption rate of employer-sponsored qualified plans has increased greatly in the past few decades. It is now the norm for a company to offer a retirement plan of some sort, whether the employer contributes beyond paying for the plan administration or not. This has increased the number of participants in the investment markets and has also contributed to the wide use of mutual funds.

Data transfer speeds have simply exploded beyond what anyone ever thought was possible. Imagine that in 1929 it took a whole minute just to transmit two hundred words across the transatlantic telegraph cable. At the 2017

International Solid-State Circuits Conference (ISSCC) in San Francisco, it was announced that researchers at Japan's Hiroshima University have developed a terahertz (THz) transmitter. They claim this new transmitter can send data at a rate ten times faster than even the fifth-generation (5G) technology that is not expected until 2020. This type of technology allows the people accessing the web for information to now receive and analyze high volumes of data nearly instantaneously to the data's inception.

Combine this with the recent revolution of quantitative analysis. Most of us know this concept from an example I used previously, the manner in which the Oakland Athletics professional baseball team built a competitive team on a shoestring budget. They did this by using analytics of mass volumes of data on every player in the major leagues. Now software engineers have written programs to enable anyone with a little bit of money, guts, and motivation to trade high volumes of securities over the Internet while sitting in the basement of their mother's house.

Then there is the advent of high-velocity trading, where the traders who employ this strategy will trade thousands of shares of securities in milliseconds, hoping to make a penny or two on each share, and then get out of the trade. In many cases now, this is not even a person executing those trades, but computers set up to process these huge amounts of data and overlay algorithms in order to make decisions and trades instantaneously. This has resulted in yet another significant increase in the number of shares traded across the worldwide market exchanges. Aldridge and Krawciw, in their book *Real-Time Risk*,[10] estimate that trading volume attributed to high-frequency trading in 2016 was anywhere between 10 and 40% of the trading volume in US equities and 10 to 15% of the trading volume overseas. These quick transactions in and out of positions have undoubtedly led to greater levels of market volatility.

No one will argue that the changes in technology and exponentially more market participation have changed the manner in which markets operate since the 1950s. The level of volatility has changed since MPT was put forth as an academic theory in 1952. For a large portion of society, absorbing such volatility and hoping it comes back in time for when they need the funds is riskier than ever. We also need to factor in that we live a lot longer than investors did in the mid-1900s. This causes us to need to fund a longer retirement as the healthier and more active people we are today.

ENTREPRENEURIAL ED

As we discussed earlier, Ed has no strategic plan for his business or his personal finances. Ed has not deployed any tools or techniques to reduce his taxes. He has been paying anywhere from $200,000 to $400,000 in federal and state

---

10 Irene Aldridge and Steven Krawciw, *Real-Time Risk: What Investors Should Know about FinTech, High-Frequency Trading and Flash Crashes* (Hoboken, NJ: Wiley, 2017).

income taxes annually, averaging well over $200,000 annually over the past ten years. He has no entity structuring. Ed and Edwina face significant capital gains today and in the future. Ed has owned many of these properties for decades. The family has been smart with their real-estate investment and fortunate in how the real-estate values in the San Francisco Bay Area have consistently risen and have come back strong from the 2008 Great Recession. However, if they need to sell any of their properties for liquidity and spending needs, which will happen one day, they will pay a large capital gains tax.

Remember, their exposure to the estate taxes is also significant. Today, they have a net worth around $25 million. If we apply just a modest level of appreciation on the real estate of the historical average of inflation at 3.75%, their net worth will be approximately $32 million in ten years, when Ed is eighty years old, and just under $44 million when Ed is ninety. If Ed and Edwina tragically passed away today, the children would be forced to sell property in order to pay an estimated $4.1 million in estate taxes and expenses within the nine-month requirement of the IRS. That's just under 20% of their net worth. If they do not make any changes to their current structure, the kids will have to come up with just over $6 million to pay estate taxes in ten years and almost $8.5 million in twenty years.

Ed and Edwina own all of their income-producing real estate personally. The only tool Ed has used to protect his wealth is to purchase a very large umbrella insurance policy to protect against liability.

I hear this a lot: "But I have insurance!" Remember, when it comes to wealth protection, we want to create as many divided sections and use as many layers of protection as the situation warrants—no more, no less.

If someone is injured at one of Ed's properties and Ed is found liable, he has to hope his insurance is sufficient and the claim is not denied. Ed also has to hope the claim by and reward to the predator does not also go beyond the coverage on that one property; the others could potentially be at risk in order to pay the claim. If Ed had arranged his affairs to include additional layers of protection, such as a business structure, employee and executive benefit plans, and so forth, he would be able to manage his situation and minimize his losses much more easily.

Now we start to bring the other concepts together. Ed and Edwina are afraid to do any estate planning, including minimal annual gifting, for fear that their two children are not making good decisions about their partners. The daughter is engaged to be married, and although Ed and Edwina like the fiancé very much, they are still not ready to do anything that could ultimately cause control or ownership of their assets to leave the family. The same goes for the son, who has a significant other whom the family is not so excited about seeing at reunions. The parents do not want this woman involved in anything that has to do with the family affairs or the real-estate business. Although there are plenty of options to reduce, or even eliminate, their estate tax liability exposure, this fear is a significant factor keeping them from implementing most of these options, thus leaving the liability in their future.

Decision-making is not a strong suit of this family, and this isn't the first generation where this is evident. You'll recall I met Ed after delivering a talk to donors of a very large nonprofit, where he approached me and eagerly told me his father made every one of the wealth predator mistakes and he thought he was making them too. This includes the inability to make decisions. Most often, Ed's decision was to not make a decision. He and Edwina have never hired an expert team to help them. He's trying to do it himself, with heavy reliance on Internet research. There is no decision-making process for things that take them out of their comfort zone. When it comes to making a decision about buying a property, Ed is quick and thorough. He would have never been able to build the real-estate portfolio he has built if it weren't for his ability to identify opportunities and proceed methodically and prudently or consciously back away. No deal is better than a bad deal.

Edwina simply lives in fear. She's frozen. Unless the tools and strategies deployed to help them are perfect, with no risk, no loss of liquidity, and no impact on their personal cash flow, she is not going to do anything. The only thing that Edwina could think of was everything that could go wrong with the plan. Every catastrophic possibility just short of a meteor hitting North America keeps her up at night. As a result, Ed and Edwina cannot take any action; they are like the ice of the procrastination glacier.

In speaking with Ed's attorney in order to effectively collaborate on the family's affairs and options, he informed me that this was not the first time Ed and Edwina had been presented with options for protecting their assets and reducing their tax liability, both income and estate tax. They were not able to make any decisions before, and the attorney was in full support of the plan options we presented.

When people like Ed and Edwina are overwhelmingly invested in real estate, they are brick rich and cash poor. Unfortunately, they cannot spend bricks. Every time they save up enough money to buy another property, they do, and leave themselves cash poorer (in the San Francisco Bay Area, that is at least a million dollars, which Ed seems to accomplish every four to five years).

Ed is only comfortable investing in real estate and therefore has no other investments. He has an asset allocation of 99% real estate and 1% cash. Therefore, he doesn't have any diversification, but he is not susceptible to stock market fluctuations, which he fears.

Ed and Edwina's overall grade in avoiding the five great wealth predators is a D.

WHAT TO DO ABOUT IT

There are many strategies available to financial planners to help people facing these wealth predators. Anything done in this arena must be aligned with the rest of your wealth and estate planning. Using this book as a guide will take you down a path to achieving the end result I'm encouraging you to construct: a careful series of complementary tools and techniques to help you achieve your overall strategy and vision for the future of your company and your family.

I have shown you how avoiding unnecessary taxes can be accomplished by not just seeking to take current deductions but also putting in place plans that will enable you to consistently reduce taxes and dedicate those resources toward rewarding your employees and simultaneously saving for your retirement, all the while protecting those assets from liability. Ed and Edwina had a great opportunity to deploy plans such as these years ago. If they had, they would likely have a large nest egg put aside.

If you are charitably inclined, there are opportunities for you to protect those assets for your use during your lifetime but leave the remainder to causes you care about deeply. If Ed had created a plan such as this, any assets put in these special trusts would also be protected from the wealth predators.

Assets can be broken up into a series of entities, such as limited liability companies (LLCs), so they are segregated from one another and from your personal assets. Operating companies can be created separately to manage the assets and handle cash flow.

Open communication and prenuptial agreements can go a long way to providing a greater level of comfort for Ed and Edwina. This comfort level will hopefully enable them to involve the children in the business and allow for implementation of strategies to take advantage of their opportunities to reduce exposure and benefit from their success even more.

Reminder: This is not tax or legal advice. Please do not go out and implement any of these ideas without prior consultation with your expert team of advisors.

SELF-ASSESSMENT

Here are some questions to ask your current or potential investment advisor:

Describe your investment style and philosophy._____

_____

Do you have options for different styles of investment management? What are they?_____

_____

How do you manage risk in your portfolios?_____

_____

What products do you use?_____

_____

Will you be managing my investment account or will you be using a centrally managed platform or other advisors?_____

_____

Including fund fees, what is the total cost of me investing with you?_____

_____

Think about what is more important for you at this stage of your life. Is it more important for you to grow the assets you are investing in the stock and bond markets, or is it more important for you to protect those assets?_____

_____

Reassess this decision every three to five years to be sure changes to your investments and the way they are being managed are still aligned with your current situation and your current tolerance for risk.

Has anything changed?_____

_____

Have there been life events or illnesses?_____

_____

Has there been a windfall or jump in wealth for any reason?

_____

Is business declining and at threat of failure?_____

_____

The common mistake here is for people to become complacent with their investments and their advisor and not review these things on a regular basis. The investment questions should be asked again at these reviews.

Big Mistake #6

FOLLOWING THE CONVENTIONAL "WISDOM" OF WALL STREET

"A trend was a trend only because people thought it so.
And in thinking it so, they made it so."

—Tom Clancy

When someone becomes a financial advisor, they are required to pass several exams that include questions about portfolio construction and management. To become a Certified Financial Planner™ professional, they must understand MPT thoroughly, as well as the technical background that substantiates the theory.

I'd like to illustrate the concept by telling you about my father's experience with MPT. My father, Sam, was a Holocaust survivor who was saved from the Nazis when his family, along with many others near where he lived in Lithuania, were abducted and placed in forced labor camps in Siberia. Their land, personal property, and businesses were stolen by the Soviets, then they were thrown into overpacked cattle cars for a month-long train trip in the most disgusting sanitation conditions you can imagine. Many people became horribly sick during the trip, and several died.

When they arrived in Siberia, the families were divided into groups to perform work for the war effort wherever they were physically able. Some were sent to the Arctic fish factories, others to manufacturing plants of all sorts, and my family was sent to the sugar factories. With three other families, they lived in a one-bedroom apartment with mattresses on the floor from wall to wall.

Sam was a young teenager who didn't quite understand everything going on around him. Just when things were as bad as you might think they could get, Sam contracted typhus. Typhus ravaged most of the concentration camps and other forced detention or labor camps across Europe, wherever there was a high concentration of people in poor sanitary conditions in small, confined areas. The labor camps and poor housing facilities and their dilapidated conditions were a prime environment for fleas and ticks to spread the deadly bacteria. Most people who contracted typhus died, including Anne Frank and her sister.

Health care didn't exist in the camps unless a person was gravely ill, so Sam's typhus was left untreated until he fell into a coma. The coma lasted three months. He was placed in isolation in a hospital until he woke up. The doctors and nurses then performed surgery to remove the infection that was, by that point, consuming his legs. There was no available anesthesia, because it was saved for the war effort, to treat injured soldiers. The doctors opened his legs to physically scrape the infectious pus material from his diseased flesh.

Sam survived, but the physical deterioration, the nerve damage caused by the disease, and the tough treatment that saved his life caused permanent damage. Although he eventually learned to walk again, this damage limited his physical abilities and made schooling much more challenging than it had been prior to getting ill. These symptoms remain with him as I write this today.

My father, his family, and his neighbors who were forced onto those trains were the lucky ones. I know it seems implausible, but yes, they were lucky. Several days after my family was kidnapped and sent to Siberia, the Nazi army invaded their town and marched every Jew into the forest and murdered them all by machine gun. Although they lost several family members in the Soviet labor camps and Nazi concentration camps, my father and my grandparents survived all of it.

Not long after their arrival at the camp, my grandfather was sentenced to eighteen months of hard labor in Stalin's Gulag. He was very ill and weak when he got out, but he still had his wits about him. As soon as the war ended, he thought about how to return to their home and his businesses. He even thought about how they could join my grandmother's brothers, who had left Europe prior to World War I and immigrated to America. With the help of these uncles in America, my father and grandparents came to the United States after WWII. Again, they were among the lucky ones who were able to do so. Many desperately tried to do the same and were unable. Many even arrived on the shores of free nations, including the United States, but were turned back.

They arrived in this great land of opportunity and wealth with literally nothing. With help from his uncles, Sam went to school, learned English, and started to work. He performed any work he could find, scrimping and scraping just to survive. For the new immigrants, this was difficult, but it was heaven compared to the hell they had just escaped in Europe. They knew they were lucky.

My father's fortunes continued when he was accepted and then attended Ohio State University, where he met my mother, Eileen, who grew up in Columbus. They married very quickly, as folks did back then; my mom was eighteen years old at the time. They moved to Chicago for my father to attend optometry school and had my sister just three years later. They were young and poor and had very little income and no savings. When I was young, I used to hear stories about how they had to choose between feeding my sister, my elder by eight years, or eating, themselves. My sister sure likes to tell me and my older brother how easy we had it when we were kids compared to her.

Sam worked hard—very hard. Eventually, he saved a little money and qualified for a micro loan, as it's called today, to start his own business. Sam purchased a small optometry practice on the South Side of Chicago. The American dream was slowly coming true. They bought one side of a small duplex in a new neighborhood in the suburbs, he had his own family, and he was an entrepreneur, just like his father was in Europe.

Be careful what you ask for in life; Sam now had to work even harder. He left his young family first thing in the morning to head into Chicago traffic for an hour and a half, saw patients all day, and returned late in the evening. The business had ups and downs with the cycles of the economy, but my parents were able to save. We didn't take very fancy vacations, and my parents didn't live high on the hog either. We weren't wealthy by any measure, but they provided for us and made sure we had what we needed.

My father is what I call, in finance language, a squirrel. We didn't know it, but somehow, all along the way, he had been saving money. We're not talking about millions, but for the amount of income he made and with three children in the house, he did quite well for himself. He had a financial advisor at one of the big, famous brokerage houses in Chicago. Over the years, the investment firm changed hands, changed names, and went through its share of scandals. At each juncture, my father stuck with the advisor and trusted what the advisor was doing for him and his investments.

FIDUCIARY (AND NON-FIDUCIARY) ADVICE

It turns out the "advisor" was more of a stockbroker and not an advisor after all. Like most financial professionals today, the advisor was not compelled to work as a fiduciary for my father or any other clients. The advisor also recommended riskier investments than were appropriate for my father's risk tolerance and for someone at my father's stage of life. The advisor only used one method of investing his clients' money, which went directly into the company's centrally managed platforms with the rest of his clients. Therefore, my parents really had no choice and were never educated on any form of investing other than MPT. The little bit of wealth my parents were able to accumulate rode the roller-coaster ride of the stock market all the way up to and even into my father's retirement, at age sixty-five.

In 1993, my father turned sixty-five and sold his practice. Now the money they saved and the proceeds from the sale of his business were going to have to be enough wealth to provide for them for the rest of their lives. These assets had to be managed prudently, with thought as to what was in the best interest of my parents and not just what was the trendy thing to do with other people's money.

The advisor didn't know much about my father and his background. He didn't ask questions deeper than what was required to understand his clients' situation and individual values system. For example, he should at least have asked, "Dr. and Mrs. Frankel, is it more important for you to grow these funds or protect them for your retirement? If you had a choice, do you prefer to spend down your hard-earned, hard-saved money, or do you prefer to pass it along to your children?" If the "advisor" were actually an advisor, he would not have taken the level of risk he took with my parents' savings.

As a result, my parents went through every bubble–burst cycle, including big bubbles like 1987's and even the deep dive of the dot-com bubble in 2001. At each dip, Sam was told by his big supermarket bank advisor, "Don't worry; it will come back."

Now, let's think about this a second. In 2001, Sam was seventy-three and had already sold his business. The days of waiting for his money to come back were over. The days of making a living in order to preserve and pass along a little bit of wealth to his heirs were over. After everything my father had lived through in his life, this was stress and anxiety he didn't need.

During my adult life, I watched my dad go through many roller-coaster rides of the markets and the economy. As a human being, I cannot do that to other people without at least educating them on other options they may find better for their situation. As professionals acting as a fiduciary for clients in all aspects of our engagement, we have to be better than that. As a businessman with an MBA, it simply makes business sense to do what is in the best interest of our clients.

In defense of my father's "advisor," like many in the

personal finance field, I was taught the same concepts in school and in training to become an advisor, all of which advocate MPT without any education or training on the alternatives. In a nutshell, you, the investor, are expected to turn over your hard-earned, hard-saved wealth to us smart professionals, and we will invest it the same way we do for everyone else. You are then expected to ride the ups and downs of the markets and the economy, and at each major trough, we are taught to say, just as Sam's advisor said, "Don't worry, it will come back."

In my observation, and with all due respect to my business school professors, I don't believe many—if any—of the theorists, whether they be academics, TV talking heads, or research analysts, have ever had to sit across the table from a client at the later stages of their life and tell them that 20, 30, or 40% of their wealth has just evaporated. They've never had to look that person in the eye and talk about how investing is risky. It's heartbreaking to have that conversation with people. It is these moments that make or break an investor's confidence in their advisor and in the system the advisor community so strongly advocates.

RISK VERSUS REWARD

There's no panacea against losses and the risk of the markets; if you're in the markets, you *are* subject to risk. However, there are a small group of advisors out there who place as much value on protecting their clients' wealth as much as—if not more than—helping those clients grow their wealth. These advisors put processes and systems in place to help mitigate volatility and losses. It may even mean reducing exposure, increasing cash in the account, and waiting on the sidelines in part or in whole until probabilities of success and less risk return.

When you've reached the stage in your business where you're doing well and you're saving money, you've hopefully created a retirement plan and have started to save and invest for your retirement and your legacy. A significant amount of your savings will most likely be in investment markets of some nature. This is when you will want to be sure you are working with a financial advisor that has taken the time to understand you, your values, and your vision and is acting in alignment with those important principles. If they have not, as in the case of my father's advisor, you will want to find someone who does.

Adopting a more dynamic strategy is not for everyone, and no investment plan is perfect; only you can decide what is most comfortable for you. Is it worth it to you to put your funds at risk for the potential of significant growth, or is it more important to you to protect your wealth? Are you willing to give up some growth for protection? That's the bottom line, because you can't have it both ways.

WHY BUY, HOLD, HOPE?

After the academic theory of 1952 brought us MPT, decades of propaganda have told us we have to stay fully invested in the markets at all times, because if we don't, we're going to miss the best days of the market. Investors are trained to have a fear of missing out. Have you ever wondered where that advice comes from?

It comes from people who most likely have a vested interest in you doing as they say, staying fully invested in the markets. After a while, if a theory is repeated enough, it becomes conventional wisdom and begins to be taught in schools. Once it is taught in schools and universities, required to pass regulatory exams without alternatives, it is cemented as dogma and implemented in firms across the globe. As this theory becomes the standard for an industry—and experts learn to make money from it—people stop asking whether it's truly the best approach for everyone. Further "education" of the public through the mass media continues to seed the future of the theory remaining the standard.

One of the legacies from the Watergate scandal of the 1970s is the phrase "follow the money." Follow the money proved to be very helpful in figuring out who had the motivation for a sloppy hotel break-in and then cover-up. Let's try that. Who benefits from the investors staying invested in the markets? Although historically low, a 2015 survey by Bankrate shows the market is huge, with 52% of Americans investing in the stock market. Most of those are invested in mutual funds.[11] Whenever there is a large market of customers such as this, there is a lot of money flying around to be grabbed by the market players at every level. There is a long list of people who make money from investing in the stock and bond markets, including brokers, dealers, market-makers, advisors, clearing firms, separate account managers, fund managers, custodians, and the corporations that develop and market investment products.

As I write this, even though the stock market is back at record highs, we are still at some of the lowest levels of invested Americans in the past couple of decades. This is true even given the previous statistics I quoted. The influx of investors I mentioned earlier peaked and then fell off dramatically after the 2008 crisis and hasn't come back since. Perhaps people are losing faith in the markets. But are they? Or are they losing faith in the professionals guiding them through the markets' cycles? Are investors just shying away from a repeat of the severe market bubbles they experienced twice in one decade, in 2001 and 2008?

The real answer is probably that people are scared. Psychologists might say they have a form of post-traumatic stress disorder. It's the old aphorism "one bitten, twice shy," or "fool me twice, shame on me." The problem is, in this case, it is not just once or even twice; the bubble–burst

---

11 http://www.bankrate.com/finance/consumer-index/money-pulse-0415.aspx

cycles seem to be happening every seven to ten years. If you've ever been bitten by a dog, you are highly likely to at least shy away from dogs afterward. The real-estate mortgage-spurred financial crisis of 2008 bit a lot of people hard. The other element at play here is most investors have not been educated on a more conservative investment process that will enable their clients to experience prudent growth but with reduced risk exposure. (Notice I didn't say no risk.) Regardless of the reason, there are a significant number of investors who have removed themselves from the equity market completely, and it has risen back to record highs without their participation—or benefit.

Back to the investigation into who benefits from MPT and the mantra of buy, hold, hope. Investment product producers of all stripes benefit from their clients staying fully invested in their products at all times. Consider the thousands of media messages sent across our eyes and ears on a daily basis encouraging us to invest in investment products of every variety. The marketing strategy employed by these companies is to rely on repetition; as I mentioned earlier, if we hear the same message over and over again consistently and over a long period, it is perceived to be fact. These companies have been advocating a philosophy of MPT for decades, and their research departments are vulnerable to biases to recommend a higher exposure to an asset class for which they produce an investment product.

The entire organizational structure is dependent on this model. There are large sales departments in these companies whose compensation is heavily dependent on a bonus structure tied to increasing investment into their products. If the company experiences a high level of conversion to cash or even distributions out of the company, it will start to affect other departments, including research, trading, and ultimately the talking heads on TV and in the executive suite.

Is this a conflict of interest with their clients? Somehow, it is not, at least as far as the regulators are concerned. But when it comes to you thinking about what is in the best interest of you and your family, you know best.

We're talking about a significant amount of money, even for low-cost products. This is investment firms' bread and butter; they rely on this income like an annuity, flowing to them on a regular basis. If you are not invested in their products, they are not able to charge all of their fees and expenses—the hidden ones too. Of course, they are going to advocate an investment philosophy that does not use cash as an investment class to protect the client's assets. This is because they cannot charge you most of their fees and will therefore suffer reduced revenues if investor balances are in cash and not in their products. If a critical mass of investors used cash for this purpose and all did so at the same time, the investment product manufacturer would no longer be a profitable concern. It's similar to a run on the bank without removing the funds from their custody. They become a free storage depot for your money; however temporary it may be, they make much less money off your money when this occurs.

In my opinion, investment firms create a significant conflict of interest with their clients when they advocate buy, hold, hope without considering economic cycles, market conditions, and the client's wealth level, vision, and life stage.

WHAT IS THE TRUE COST OF OWNING AN INVESTMENT PRODUCT?

I shocked a prospective client with our cost analysis of their portfolio when we illustrated what I call the *true cost of ownership* of their engagement with their current advisor at one of the large US supermarket bank brokerage firms. Using the independent firm Personal Fund, we realized something we have seen in numerous portfolios. On average, the published fees are usually 50% of the total fees incurred by the investor. According to Gregory Kadlec, from the Pamplin College of Business of Virginia Tech University study published in the *Financial Analysts Journal*, mutual funds' published expense ratios account for less than half of the average fund's expenses paid by the customer.[12] An investor would have to dig into the prospectus in order to find there are other expenses that will be passed along to the investor. Most of these additional costs come from the fund manager's trading costs and short-term capital gains. Yes, even though they are advocating you buy and hold, they are

---

12 http://www.cfapubs.org/doi/pdf/10.2469/faj.v69.n1.6

not. They are trading in the fund based on their research and their needs to cover fund flows and expenses. On top of those fees, there are often fees for loads; some are charged on the front of the transaction, when you buy, and others are based on when you sell the investment, back-end charges. So if the investment advisor's published expense ratio is 1%, according to the Pamplin College study, we have to add another 1% on average. Now we're at 2% annually, just to own this investment. If the advisor is charging a fee for their service, that will probably be another 1–1.5%. All right, so now you generally know your total cost of the engagement with your advisor based on the instruments they are using for your investments; in this case, it is mutual funds. On a $1 million account invested in a growth model with an 80% equity allocation, the cost of that portion of your portfolio is $16,000 annually ($1,000,000 × 80% × 2% = $16,000) to the investment product manufacturer. Think of those expenses as a boat anchor being dragged behind your investments. The investments are going to have to work much harder to achieve the same results as a portfolio with much less weight being dragged behind it. Notice that we only calculated the equity portion of their account; we'd have to add the fixed income component as well.

What happens if you move some of that money to cash? They won't make a lot of those fees. If we multiply by the hundreds or thousands of investors investing billions of dollars with a firm and across the marketplace, the loss to the company is quite substantial. Of course they're going to tell you to always leave your money in the market. The investment product manufacturers are companies I am not permitted to mention, for compliance reasons, but suffice it to say these are the companies you see advertising on TV, in magazines, and on just about every finance website and blog you can think of. For you do-it-yourselfers, do your research to know who owns the mutual fund company you are investing in. It may or may not matter to you, but you will want to know if the funds have a different brand name than the bank, insurance company, or investment company whose name you may be more familiar with. Regulatory requirements for disclosures take care of much of this for these companies, but these are lengthy documents in small print on tissue paper that most of us do not even open.

No one can time the market perfectly. If anyone tells you they can, you should run. However, if you're willing to give up a little bit of growth in exchange for some protection, there are investment advisors who have a process to help. But you can't have it both ways. This type of investing has the potential to beat appropriate benchmarks over the long term, not over any arbitrary (particularly, short) time frame. In order to fully evaluate an investment philosophy and process, the investor has to see data and participate in this process over a full market cycle. Market cycles vary in length. It can be anywhere from five to ten years or more before we see a market go from peak to trough to peak.

BUY, HOLD, HOPE FOR ENTREPRENEURS

Once an entrepreneur reaches a point of success that allows them to implement planning tools and techniques designed to take advantage of their success, they will undoubtedly implement strategies that put their capital at risk in MPT. More likely than not, this exposure will lie in employee and executive benefit plans.

Pension plans are a good example. There are many types of plans to put into your business, and many of them can be done in combination with others; it can get very complex.

Traditional pension plans operate on an actuarial computation using your age, the age of your employees if you have any, and an assumed growth rate. The growth rate is not normally assumed to be very high, perhaps 5% annually, because, according to the IRS and Department of Labor rules and regulations, regarding "qualified" plans, we must follow tables that limit the amount we're allowed to save within the plan. This actuarial computation is reviewed and adjusted annually with the plan reporting.

A common mistake people make in managing pension plan accounts is in the level of risk they take. The strategy of using a pension plan for your business is to reduce taxes, provide a nice benefit for loyal employees, protect wealth from liability and creditors, and save for your future. It is vital as the owner of a closely held business to understand that when you implement a retirement plan, the owner (you) will most likely be the trustee of the plan, making you a fiduciary for your employees. You are compelled to manage that plan in the best interests of the participants. In a properly designed plan, the owner is the primary beneficiary and participant of the plan, but if there are other participants in the plan, the fiduciary responsibilities become even more important. As a fiduciary, you must act as a prudent investor when administering the plan.

The term prudent investor actually means something quite significant and is important to understand. The Uniform Prudent Investor Act (UPIA), passed in 1994, revamped the rules that now govern the actions of trustees. The UPIA states that trustees are required to pursue an investment strategy taking into account such factors as risk and return. The UPIA provides a reasonable approach to the investment of trust assets that better meets the needs of beneficiaries while preserving trust assets.

So here's my question: If the assumptions used to create the plan are relatively modest and the goals of the plan are as I described above, why do so many people take high risks and shoot for returns commensurate with an aggressive benchmark? Don't forget, if you expect market-like or better returns, you have to expect market-like or greater risk and volatility along the way. Investors should take as little risk as possible to achieve the desired results over the long run.

Every year a plan is active in the business, a review must be completed to determine whether the plan is properly funded per the details of the plan document. If your plan's investment performance exceeds the assumptions, you will not be able to contribute as much the following year. This is not good when you, as the owner, rely on these contributions to provide tax deductions you have come to rely upon. That could present a nasty surprise next time you do your taxes without those deductions. On the other hand, if the performance is far below the plan's assumptions, you may be required to make larger contributions in the following year. Yes, this will provide for greater tax deductions, but if you have not planned for that in your cash flow, it may be challenging.

So you see, when striving for a greater return in a pension plan, we are not just taking on more market risk; we also risk our pension plans being dramatically underfunded or overfunded. We've seen this on a grander scale when public employee pension plans and large corporate pension plans (a dying breed) declined significantly during the dot-com bubble of 2001 and again during the real-estate and financial crisis of 2008.

We need to find the happy medium in there somewhere. Every fiduciary who is responsible to manage the assets of the firm, including the assets in the firm's employee benefit plans, will want to understand the differences between an MPT approach using the classic strategic investment process of buy, hold, rebalance and a grow and protect plan using dynamic asset allocation in striving to reduce risk and volatility. Neither is perfect and both are not necessarily appropriate for everyone.

Your personal index

If left unchecked, the conventional wisdom of Wall Street is a threat to your wealth. This is especially true as you reach the later stages of your career and have already built significant wealth.

For most people, there is an appeal to having more and more money, but we have to ask ourselves at what cost and at what risk we are willing to use the wealth we have already built to create more wealth. People often compare their investment performance to those of their friends, relatives, neighbors, colleagues, and members of their congregations. People also often compare their performance to an arbitrary index, time frame, or some other benchmark they have learned to follow over the years.

I prefer for you to think of what your situation is, what your risk tolerance is, and how much you need to grow your money to achieve your vision for your legacy. This will become your personal index—a benchmark for your investment goals. Your advisor should then make recommendations and act to invest with the goal of achieving your personal index. If, over any full market cycle, you do not achieve your goal, you will need to reevaluate your index and your investment strategy. If you overachieve, you will need to be sure you are not taking more risk than you are comfortable taking in order to achieve those results.

We humans generally seem to suffer from short-term memory. We quickly forget the market crashes of 1987, 1992, 2001, and 2008. I do not want you to be scared frozen, but I also do not want you to be complacent. History has a way of repeating itself; we just don't know when. Are you deploying a strategy to help mitigate those severe dips while having your money work for you in a prudent fashion?

Wealthy people fear losing their wealth too

Think about what was happening in the economy and stock markets around the world in 2005. It was boom time: "full employment," record returns in the markets, and most people returned to the markets from the dot-com bubble burst of 2001.

In 2005, Russ Alan Prince conducted a study in which they asked people with a net worth of at least $1 million if losing their wealth was a significant fear in their lives. What percentage of respondents do you think replied yes?

Answer: 90%.

If 90% of the respondents answered yes in a booming economy, how many do you think would have harbored this fear directly after the real-estate bubble burst in 2008 and in the subsequent severe recession? The mere thought of having to cut back on their lifestyle or to not achieve their vision for retirement is horrifying for wealthy people. The thought of losing everything they have worked so hard to achieve is devastating. The thought of not achieving their legacy for their families or the causes for which they have deep passion is very disturbing. This is the fear many wealthy people feel as they wake up at 2:00 in the morning.

Why take unnecessary risk when you do not need that amount of risk to achieve your vision? If you cannot answer with a high level of comfort for you and your spouse, I invite you to step back and think about your current investment strategy and its tactical processes. Come back to the all-important why. Will your current investment strategy potentially cause your greater why to not be achieved?

Health-care professionals

Health-care professionals have unique risks and thus interesting opportunities we need to spend some time discussing. I want to stress the importance of these professionals taking this threat seriously by understanding the magnitude of the problem.

The level of litigation that has hit the medical community in the past few decades has not abated. According to the New England Journal of Medicine's 2006 survey,[13] approximately 80% of all claims in the United States come from obstetrics, surgery, a missed or delayed diagnosis, and mistakes with the prescribing of medication.

Nineteen percent of the defendants were obstetricians–gynecologists, 17% were general surgeons, and 16% were primary-care physicians. Other high-risk specialties included ophthalmologists and anesthesiologists. For years, there have been challenges in the courts to reduce

---

13 http://www.nejm.org/doi/full/10.1056/NEJMsa054479#t=articleResults

frivolous lawsuits, but still, in 37% of the cases, no adverse outcome from the medical care was even evident. Furthermore, just because a medical professional makes an error, it does not translate into malpractice. There's an old joke in Chicago that if you look hard enough, you can find a judge to indict a ham sandwich.

There are serious claims requiring indemnification and, in some cases, punitive restitution. Fifty-six percent of the claims received compensation, at an average payout of $485,348, of which the claims resolved by actually going to court resulted in an average payout of $799,365.

Specialties with high-capital equipment requirements, such as ophthalmologists, dentists, and some diagnostic specialties requiring very expensive tools and equipment, have particular risks and opportunities. Most independent medical professionals have opportunities to develop multiple entities to hold different assets in order to silo some from others.

Please take these threats and opportunities seriously by following the advice here to seek guidance to understand your current circumstances, risks, options, and opportunities to minimize threats and optimize your unique situation.

ENTREPRENEURIAL ED

Entrepreneurial Ed only has illiquid investments and therefore doesn't have any investments outside his real-estate assets, so we cannot discuss how he invested his funds. He did not take advantage of the opportunities of the market, but he also didn't risk his assets in it. It's a wash. Or is it?

WHAT TO DO ABOUT IT

There is the opportunity cost of how Ed managed his real-estate business, most especially his tax strategy within the business. This is actually quite common for small- to medium-sized real-estate investors like Ed. These smart people start to build a real-estate portfolio and seek to optimize tax deductions through depreciation and interest deductions. Their background and their spheres of influence are adept at identifying and negotiating smart real-estate deals and not necessarily in structuring and managing a business.

I would like to see the real-estate investors, as well as most other business owners in other industries, examine how they can structure their businesses so they may take full advantage of executive and employee benefit programs. Many of these programs allow for significant contributions that are tax deductible, greatly reducing their tax burden far beyond what most think.

Let's take a look at how things might have been different for Entrepreneurial Ed if he had started a defined benefit pension plan in his business ten years ago. Assuming Ed saved $100,000 in a tax-deductible defined benefit pension plan for ten years and averaged an annual return of 5.0% per year, he and his family theoretically would have the following saved and protected:

	Without DB plan (estimated)	With DB plan (estimated)
Liquid net worth at end of 10 years	$2,200,000	$3,500,000
Liquid net worth at age 90	$2,300,000	$3,900,000
Taxes paid through age 90	$4,700,000	$3,000,000

As you can see, while nothing is guaranteed, it appears as though Ed would have benefited greatly by having a pension plan in his business. Even more of a benefit in Ed's situation is that he does not have any W-2 employees. This translates into him receiving 100% of the benefits in the plan. Other plan designs could be implemented if he did have employees or for when his children get involved in the business.

Now that Ed is in the situation he is in without any of these plans, we have to consider other arrangements for him outside the business. Some of those options are not officially plans at all but, rather, the clever use of trusts, charitable giving, and insurance products that may provide a dual benefit for him and his family.

There are many criteria to determine which type of plan is most appropriate and suitable for you and your company. Some strategies and plans do not provide for current tax deductions but provide for income that is taxed less or not taxed at all when you begin to take distributions.

SELF-ASSESSMENT

In the previous section, I provided you with several questions to ask about investment style, but first, before you ask the advisor anything, I want you to ask yourself if the advisor is taking time to get to know you and your spouse. Observe and evaluate their approach to take you through a process to determine if you're a good mutual fit.

Do they understand your background?_____

_____

Did they inquire as to how you built your success—i.e., did you inherit, or did you scrimp and scrape to get where you are today?_____

_____

Do they ask about your parents and what their background is and how it impacts you today?_____

_____

Do they go beyond the risk tolerance questionnaire from their company to ask you questions that make you think and even feel what it would be like if you lost as much as 50% of your investments?_____

_____

Are they demonstrating they have a clear process rather than shooting from the hip in getting to know you and managing your wealth?_____

_____

Do they discuss how they manage risk and strive to also protect your wealth?_____

_____

HOW TO PROTECT YOURSELF FROM THE WEALTH PREDATORS

Avoiding the five wealth predators of the affluent should be a constant exercise for any prudent person, especially business owners. Picture the Pentagon; you are building a series of concentric walls that would make it difficult for an aggressive attorney to get to the pot of gold—your assets—in the center. Furthermore, you can section off part of your business or certain assets from one another to keep them protected in the event one of them comes under attack. Most attorneys will take a look at such a structure and tell their client it isn't worth it to go after you, because the structure alone will limit the amount any plaintiff may be able to collect. They saw your defensive posture and moved on to chase other prey.

In addition to being constantly aware and hiring the

right team, I want you to use this book as a guide to avoid the predators. If you go back through the book and follow the recommendations to review your options in each of these areas and ask the right questions of yourself and your advisor team, then you are more likely to limit your exposure to the predators. This is not meant to be an exhaustive list, but it will give you a good start.

Am I exposed to lawsuits from a disgruntled customer, vendor, or employee?_____

_____

To what degree am I exposed?_____

_____

What is exposed?_____

_____

How much will my current insurance cover?_____

_____

What are some strategies to reduce my exposure?_____

_____

Can you illustrate these strategies into a financial plan?_____

_____

What are the risks in these strategies?_____

_____

What are the costs?_____

_____

Can they be changed or reversed once implemented?_____

_____

Remember, no plan is perfect, and there will be costs. Your goal is to engage your team so you fully understand your current situation; obtain options to improve your situation; learn the advantages, disadvantages, exit strategies, and cost; then make a timely decision. If you wait for the perfect situation with no cost and no risk, you will not make decisions and will not take action to improve your situation to protect your business and your wealth.

_____

The bad news is that most likely, if you are reading this, you are an outlier. You are working toward or have already achieved a level of success that is far above average. Unfortunately, this makes you a target for a system of people who seek to siphon a great degree of your success away from you.

The good news is there are things you can do to mitigate or remove a great degree of these risks. In many cases, the strategies you can deploy will not only protect you from some predators but will provide an opportunity to take advantage and benefit from the situation.

The first step is understanding your current risk.

Big Mistake #7

NO BUSINESS TRANSITION PLANNING

"Look on every exit as being an entrance somewhere else."
—Tom Stoppard, *Rosencrantz and Guildenstern Are Dead*

According to Chris Snyder's foreword in *The $10 Trillion Opportunity*, "The United States Small Business Administration estimates that only 20% of privately held businesses available for sale each year are successfully sold. More startling, twelve months after selling, 75% of business owners profoundly regretted their decision."

Consider this: Due to the age of baby boomers, it is estimated that up to $10 trillion in business value will change hands in the next twenty years. It only makes sense, given that, in the United States alone, 10,000 people turn sixty-five years old every day. Do you intend to transition your business in that market environment? What is going to happen to your business when you retire or pass away?

Are you prepared personally, professionally, and psychologically? Do you have an exit plan?

Nowhere is it more important to keep more of what you make than at this moment. This will most likely be the most important business transaction of your career. You have put your heart and soul—not to mention your cash and sweat—into your business for years, perhaps decades. How are you going to not just recoup that investment but optimize its value for you to monetize?

If you're in this position, you've made some smart decisions along the way to have a thriving business. You've persevered through myriad challenges, including staff turnover, partner challenges, losing customers, recessions, broken equipment, and vendor issues, among other problems. There have likely been cycles in your business that have created other stresses and challenges that you've navigated as best as possible. You can now enjoy great times with friends and family and live a comfortable lifestyle in a nice home.

It is time to start planning for the next phase of ownership for this business and for your life after the handover. It's time to develop a transition plan. Transition planning for your business should actually occur several years before you intend to reduce your role or exit completely. I recommend you think about the transition of your business when you form your business. This helps shift your frame of mind, so you can be ready for the next phases far ahead of time, thus reducing the psychological transition phase.

The type of planning will depend greatly on the type of

business you have, the structure of your business, and who the constituents are who have a vested interest in the outcome of the transition. A transition can take many forms, from a one-time liquidity event, to a payment period, to a stock trade, to a gifting program, and any combination of those and other strategies that may be appropriate for your situation. For some, a transition of their business is simply not possible, and the business ends when the principals stop their work.

Here is a summary of the types of transitions most popular for private company transitions depending on internal versus external buyers:

IPO

If you have built a firm that would be attractive to the mass investing public, selling a portion of your company in the public markets may be an attractive option for you. Likely, you and key management would need to stay in place for several years post-IPO. Going through an IPO process is quite complicated and would introduce a great deal of regulatory requirements many owners are not willing to deal with. The nature of the company changes as well. Rather than being a closely held business where the details of the firm are kept private, for public companies the levels of transparency and accountability change substantially. The IPO is an outlier in the options for most small- to mid-sized business owners.

Sale to outside party

Your business may very well be an ideal acquisition for another individual or company. Frequently, there are customers or vendors in your supply chain for which your company may be a complementary fit. Often, there are synergies with other firms that may make the combined firm more efficient and effective than they are separate by finding areas over commonality that may reduce costs and increase margins.

Sale to management

You may have competent and passionate management in your firm who would be ideal to continue your business. Quite often, management buyouts will require that the owner finance some of the sale over a period of time. The benefits of a management buyout are that there is a smooth transition, customers already know the team, and most employees will stay on with the new ownership.

Employee stock option plan (ESOP)

An ESOP is a type of plan that begins to give stock ownership in the company to the employees of the company. It is a way for a business owner to reward loyal employees, create a market for their stock, and slowly transition themselves out of the business. Owners who use such plans normally have a long-term workforce that takes pride in the brand and its products and services. Giving ownership only increases that loyalty with a true sense of ownership by the team.

Transition to next generation

This may be the trickiest option of them all. First, is there an appropriate candidate who understands the business, has the business acumen to continue the business, has a passion for the business, is respected by management and employees, and wants to take over the business? The next challenge is usually a valuation process and then, finally, a means of funding a transition. Parents will have to consider their liquidity needs to be sure they are not agreeing to some sort of payout over time in an installment sale or by financing the buyout completely in a way they cannot afford. How will this be offset with other heirs who are not involved in the business?

Let it die

One option is to optimize current income and siphon as much value out of the business presently and then just close the doors when you're done. This has ramifications with income tax and potential exposure to future liabilities if not done correctly, but some businesses simply do not have the value to be transitioned to another party.

Unfortunately, according to the EPI,[14] this is another area where statistics of people planning ahead and doing the most important deal of their lives are not impressive:

☐ 67% of owners are not familiar with .all exit options

☐ 78% have no formal transition team

☐ 83% have no written transition plan

☐ 49% have done no planning at all

☐ 93% have no formal life-after plan

☐ 40% have no plans in place to cover illness, death, or forced exit

☐ 50% feel ownership transition plans require the company to remain profitable for plans to be properly executed, yet . . .

☐ 86% have not taken on a strategic review or a value enhancement project

☐ 56% feel they have a good idea of what their business was worth, but only . . .

☐ 18% have had a formal valuation in the past two years

---

14 Exit Planning Institute (EPI), "2013 Exit Planning Institute State of Owner Readiness Report," https://ox242.infusionsoft.com/app/form/2013-soor-request-form

WHEN TO START? NOW!

Several years prior to wanting to execute a transition, the principals of a closely held business (you and your other stakeholders) will want to optimize the value of the business. Creating greater value by building a strong team, streamlining operations, reducing costs, enhancing value-added services in the marketplace, improving brand awareness, and taking greater market share will bring a higher value, equity, and ultimately price. These are all the actions you can identify so you can then push and pull the levers of enterprise value. If price is determined as a multiple of one data point and is normally found to be in a certain range for similar businesses, increasing the value and efficiency of your business will put your ultimate value multiplier at the top end of the range.

Beginning a transition plan far in advance also enables you to be sure you have the structuring in place to enhance value and makes for a smoother transition. Certain kinds of structuring will be more beneficial in the taxes the seller will incur. Some structuring is less generous to you and more generous to the tax man.

The right time to pull the trigger to initiate your transition choice requires the optimal alignment of the right timing of each of the following:

☐ Personal financial planning, so you are sticking with your vision planned out years ago

☐ Psychological planning and preparation, to be sure you are as ready as possible for the next phase of your life (This shouldn't be taken lightly.)

☐ Business planning and preparation after a value-enhancement effort

☐ The market cycle

If alliance partners or employees are part of the transition, they can be trained and better prepared to take over the reins. In a transition to the next generation, this gives significant time not only for training but also for the next generation to establish themselves as leaders and to build credibility with the team in advance of the turnover of power.

Multigenerational planning may be the most challenging of transitions. This is especially true if there are multiple children and is an even greater challenge if some children are involved in the business and some are not.

A national survey of the heirs of failed businesses was conducted by Karen File, an associate professor at the University of Connecticut's Business School, and Russ Alan Prince of Prince and Associates for their book on family businesses.[15] They found that 90% of businesses fail to go to the next generation because of inadequate estate planning. Eight out of ten parents had a current estate plan at

---

15 Russ Alan Prince and Karen Maru File, *Marketing to the Family Business Owners: A Toolkit for Life Insurance Professionals* (National Underwriter Company, 1995).

death . . . or so they thought. All too often, the plan was out of date for the current circumstances.

Furthermore, they found that only one in three businesses actually goes on to the next generation, only one in eight goes to the third generation, and only three in a hundred—3%—goes on to the fourth generation. Now, not all of that is because of a bad plan. Probably more comes from not having a plan at all or from not having interested and competent heirs to transition the business.

Regardless of whether your business is going to the next generation or going to be sold, planning far in advance will make for a better experience for everyone involved. You would hate to have worked your butt off for years, only to have your business leave the family because of a lack of planning or your heirs be forced to sell your pride and joy in a fire sale because you did not optimize its value for a sale. There is no way you want that confusion and lost opportunity to be your legacy.

PLAN FOR YOUR FAMILY

A lack of planning also threatens family harmony. In any estate-planning process, it is important to have a family meeting with the adult children to explain the plan for transitioning the estate once the parents have died. The more complex the estate, the more critical this family meeting is. In working with dozens and dozens of clients over the years, one of the things parents fear most in their estate planning is that their children will question their decisions. No one wants their children or grandchildren to say, after you've died or can no longer fix the problem, "Mom and Dad, what were you thinking?"

The best way to avoid this post-mortem questioning is to first have a well-thought-out business transition and estate plan. From there, we strongly encourage clients to have that family meeting to help the rest of the family understand how the wills and trusts work, who will do what, and how the business transition and estate plan will affect each of them. If one of the members of your expert team of advisors has become the quarterback, they will most likely be the best person to present the plan. The presentation should include what will happen in the case of certain life events. Everyone should understand their role and who to call for which activity. What is the plan for long-term care needs? What are the preparations and wishes for final interment? Who will take the lead on processing the estate and communicating between all the parties? How will the business continue to serve its customers and seamlessly continue operations?

Be as detailed as possible in this process, and do not assume anything. If there is an agreement about who will take over board seats, management functions, sales activities, and financial management, be sure it is written down and communicated clearly and openly.

SUCCESS DOESN'T MEAN THEY HAVE A GOOD PLAN

In many famous cases, some of the most successful people in our society have poorly planned their business and estate legacies, have let their plans become out of date, or have not planned at all. Here again, we tend to think the most successful people in our community are very smart, have the best advisors, and must have already planned effectively to have achieved such success. Yet again, and far too often, this is a completely false assumption.

The Miami Dolphins' late owner, Joe Robbie, is famous not only for the football team but also for the stadium that carried his name until 1996. The life of Joe Robbie is a classic rags-to-riches American success story. He was born and raised in a small town in South Dakota. During the Depression, he dropped out of high school to leave home for work as a lumberjack, sending money home to help his family. He later obtained his high school diploma and worked his way into college, ending up with a degree from the University of South Dakota. Robbie enlisted in the navy the day after the Japanese attack on Pearl Harbor, and he participated in major battles, earning the Bronze Star. He earned his law degree, taught economics, was a member of Congress, and ran for governor of South Dakota. He ran a very successful law firm in South Dakota and then Minnesota.

In 1965, Robbie led a team of investors with comedian Danny Thomas to start a new NFL franchise in Miami, and the Miami Dolphins football empire was born. He built a dynasty football operation and achieved a perfect 17–0 season in 1972, with two Super Bowl victories. He was a leader in the NFL ownership group and was instrumental in many of the rule changes and innovations in the NFL. His iconic stadium was one of the first major multi-use stadiums in the United States. It was originally designed with soccer in mind, and he later owned soccer teams of the North American Soccer League and successfully created a model used for many decades to come in stadium design.

Robbie was an extremely bright and accomplished man who worked incredibly hard: a small-town high school dropout who became a prominent attorney and owner of one of the most prestigious professional sports teams in history. He also left a complete mess behind when he suddenly died in 1990—a huge and very costly mess I am sure was not part of the legacy he wanted to leave behind. His family fought about it for years and is estimated to have lost $47 million to taxes.

I'm sure Robbie's success meant he had great advisors helping him—or did he? Maybe he didn't, or maybe he didn't listen to their sage advice. According to a 2015 *Sports Illustrated* article,[16] while lying in his hospital bed in 1989, Robbie reportedly told his wife he just needed five more years in order for his plan to work. Unfortunately, he

---

16 http://www.si.com/nfl/2015/11/24/miami-dolphins-super-bowl-joe-robbie
   -stadium

died less than a year later. Much of the plans he had were never implemented or were done in secret, so the rest of the family didn't know what was done or what was planned. At his passing, there were numerous media reports that his children were shocked at how they were each relegated to smaller roles with less responsibility and an even smaller share of ownership, due to a partial sale prior to Robbie's passing. Many of these changes were warranted, given the highly publicized problems his family had with competently managing the family's enterprises. The case was in the courts for years. The football team and the stadium had to be sold. A final estate tax return with payment of any taxes owed is due to the IRS within nine months of the deceased's passing. The children paid a massive amount of taxes and attorneys' fees and ended up destroying their own relationships over the fight. It was ugly, wasteful, and unnecessary.

I could go on with more stories of famous and successful people who didn't update their plan, who planned poorly, or who did not plan at all, and as a result, their families paid the price, but I think you get the point.

I cannot overemphasize the importance of a transition plan for your business. It ensures that you do not leave a nightmare for your partners and heirs to deal with in your absence. If you have obtained a level of wealth that allows you and your family to live a nice lifestyle, you have an obligation to also be responsible in retirement, old age, and death.

ENTREPRENEURIAL ED

After Ed came up to me at the end of my speech and told me his father made every one of these mistakes and he thought he was too, we stayed and chatted for a few minutes. Ed was eager to tell me what the experience was like to settle his father's estate. He described the frustration and loss of time dealing with his father's financial affairs. Ed and his sister never got along very well, but the fighting went to a new level when their father died and left them to deal with his estate. Ed was completely overwhelmed with the process and the cost. They were forced to sell some real estate so they could pay the estate tax within nine months. You see, Dad was real-estate rich and cash poor, which left the estate without liquidity for estate taxes. Ed's a chip off the old block. I asked Ed if he knew what Form 706 was. He laughed and told me he was intimately familiar with Form 706. With its thirty-one pages of fun, Form 706 is the US Estate and Generation-Skipping Transfer Tax Return (AKA, the final tax return for You, Inc.). The real fun in Form 706 is the instructions for properly completing the form. The instructions themselves are fifty-three pages of elusive IRS language.

We presented an estate plan to Ed and Edwina, who brought their son (age twenty-six) and daughter (age thirty-one) to learn about the family's wealth and have them participate in the process. This was Ed's first step in making sure he did not handle his estate in the same manner as his father. Ed didn't know about his father's wealth and the arrangement of his estate until after his father died. He had to scramble to simultaneously figure things out while he had to manage the business and administer the estate settlement process.

When presenting a plan, I first need to understand the current situation. I start by organizing all of the assets and liabilities to be sure to understand their structures and tax status. When we first brought up the couple's net worth statement during the presentation, you could hear the daughter's exclamations from our closed-door conference all the way out into the reception area. With jaw dropped, the daughter squealed, "You're worth almost $25 million? What are you doing to protect that?"

Like Ed when he was a young man, she knew the family had wealth. She never wanted for goodies or a nice lifestyle and knew it didn't just come from nowhere. She just didn't realize it was this much. Now that she is informed, she wants to know the plan to preserve this so they don't lose their big pot of gold making their lives so wonderful.

The planning process is starting to work here. The people involved are getting informed about their current situation. There is accountability to help the process move forward. However, let me give a word of caution: Do not involve the family until you are ready to make some decisions. The family now, especially the decision-makers, understand the cost of not taking action. They understand their options along with the advantages and disadvantages of those options. They are ready and empowered to make informed decisions about what is best for them and the people and causes they care about deeply.

Real-estate investors have particular challenges when it comes to transitioning their business and its portfolio. If there are not obvious heirs to take over the management of the portfolio of properties, the parents could be leaving it to people who are not equipped to handle the responsibility. This has the potential to erode value and the ultimate legacy left behind. Ed is in such a situation. It does not appear as though either of his children are interested in learning how to manage his business, and he should consider options to simplify his holdings before it is too late.

One option is for him to complete 1031 tax-qualified exchanges with a couple of properties now and then review in another two to three years to see if it makes sense to do more. In a 1031 exchange, you are permitted to sell your highly appreciated property as long as you follow the many rules and timing; you can then buy another income property and pay no capital gains taxes. Many investors who are now in their sixties and older do not want to manage property any longer. They want the hassles of dealing with tenants, maintenance problems, vacancies, property management companies, and everything else that goes into owning and managing real estate out of their lives. It is important for real estate investors to regularly analyze the performance of their holdings. This is normally done by evaluating their capitalization rate, or "cap" rate. This is calculated by dividing the net income from the property before debt service by the current fair market value of the property. If the percentage result of this calculation falls below industry benchmarks or your expectation for your investments, then you will want to consider some options to improve this situation.

More and more, we are seeing clients go into institutional real estate with a group of other investors. This enables qualified investors to get into these investments and participate in large projects with investment-grade tenants or other types of properties that they otherwise would not have the resources to purchase or manage on their own. Of course, these investments have their own set of advantages, disadvantages, and risks, but it is certainly something people like Ed and Edwina will want to consider.

SELF-ASSESSMENT

With permission from EPI, I have inserted the following pages from their publication *Are You Ready?*[17] This will give you a basis for understanding the steps in the process to plan and execute an optimal business transition to either an outside party or an inside replacement.

---

17 Exit Planning Institute (EPI), "Are You Ready?," https://www.
    floridacapitalbank.com/sites/default/files/Are%20you%20Ready_EPI.pdf

ARE YOU READY?
TEN WAYS TO CHECK IF YOU ARE

By Christopher M. Snider, CEPA

President and CEO

Exit Planning Institute

In preparation of the questions for the State of the Owner Readiness Survey, one of the team members asked me what seemed like an obvious question, "what does 'ready' mean; how do we define 'ready'?" That seemed like a simple and obvious question that deserved an answer. So below is a set of 10 simple statements to help owners determine what they need to accomplish to be prepared or "ready" to transition their businesses. Use this as simple checklist.

You are "Prepared" or "Ready" to transition your business if you . . .

☐   Have spent some time and money getting educated on the process of how to transition your business. You have discussed transitioning with your loved ones.

☐   Your personal, financial, and business goals are aligned meaning they are defined, co-dependent, and linked.

☐   You have created an advisory team which includes at minimum: an attorney, CPA, CFP, exit advisor, spouse or partner or other family who is a "significant other" in your life. Other advisors that may be included: personal friends and advisors, banking advisor, M&A attorney, estate planning attorney, real-estate attorney, business attorney, ESOP specialist, tax specialist, insurance specialist, foundation / charity, key employees, investment banker or business broker, board members, family or personal counselor.

☐ You have created a contingency plan which should include buy-sell instructions, appropriate insurance, and specifies what should happen if before you transition something was to happen outside of your control that would prevent you from operating your business or unwillingly force you to transition. You have reviewed this plan with your trusted advisors including family members and/or partners if applicable.

☐ You have completed a strategic analysis, business valuation, and personal, financial, and business assessment(s) within the last year.

☐ You have considered all of your exit options and optimum deal structure and weighed the pros and cons of each in relation to your stated goals and objectives.

☐ Your transition plan is written and includes goals and objectives, clearly defined tasks and accountabilities, definition of your transition team, definition of your transition process, a plan leader or project manager, timelines, a budget, and your role before and after transition. This plan ideally has a multi-year implementation timeline.

☐ You have considered and designed a post business life-after plan. This plan is linked or part of your wealth management plan which has been prepared by a professional financial advisor and, if applicable, estate planning attorney, insurance specialist, tax specialist, and charitable foundation specialist.

☐ You have a pre-transition value enhancement / preliminary due diligence project underway to de-risk the business, maximize its value, minimize taxes upon transition, and improve the probability of a smooth transition to the next owner including family, partners, or employees if applicable. Family transitions should be treated no differently than other transition options. This plan ideally has a multi-year implementation timeline.

☐ You have a management program underway to ensure the post-transition leadership is prepared to operate the company after you exit and secured the appropriate specialists to handle your desired transition option.

Big Mistake Bonus!

PROCRASTINATION

"I was going to join Procrastinators Anonymous but
just never got around to it."
—Anonymous

I know I advertised there were seven mistakes, but there is one more thing I must warn you to avoid. By far, the most insidious mistake people make—and you've seen me hinting about it all along the way—is this procrastination glacier.

None of us is immune to procrastination. How we shake ourselves out of it, whatever the issue is at the moment, is anyone's guess. What is going to shake you out of it? What motivates you to take action?

The problem is we tend to stay in our comfort zone. We come up with every excuse in the world. It really doesn't help our families, our employees. It doesn't help any of our customers. Most of all, it doesn't help us, our vision, or our legacy. A lot of people live in fear or want total control. We think we know more than we do. A lot of people don't want to pay advisors and, instead, try to plan on their own, without expert guidance.

I encourage you to get out of your comfort zone. I know it's getting repetitious, but here is when I want you to think about your why. Why did you start your business? Why do you do what you do? Stay focused on that. Refer back to the exercises you've completed throughout the book. How can you best follow the path to your why?

Would you like to read your own obituary? Be careful what you ask for. Do you want to read your own obituary and know what is going to be said about you when you are gone? This guy did. He woke up one day in a Paris hotel, popped open the newspaper, and there it was in the obituaries: He was dead. True story. He didn't like what he read. He was embarrassed about what he read, about how people looked at him and his life and what little he did in his life. From that point forward, he decided he was going to change the way he lived his life. He was going to start giving back. He changed and he made a difference in the world. Who am I talking about?

Alfred Nobel.

Alfred Nobel. He took that tragic event that actually killed his brother and went on to stabilize the chemicals that eventually created dynamite. His obituary only talked about this horrible destructive man-killing thing he created. Dynamite has also done a lot of good things, but that's not what the obituary talked about.

He was in a unique position to do something about it. Most likely you won't have the opportunity to read your own obituary or hear your own eulogy. Perhaps you should take some time to sit and write what you think would be written about you if you died today. The next step is to write what you want it to say . . . yes, think with the end in mind and then go out and make it happen. Have you done what you need to do in order to make that vision a reality? This procrastination glacier, I want to encourage you to get off of it. Marianne Williamson's *A Return to Love* puts this idea eloquently:

> Our deepest fear is not that we are inadequate. Our deepest fear is that we are powerful beyond measure. It is our light, not our darkness that most frightens us . . . Your playing small does not serve the world. There is nothing enlightened about shrinking so that other people will not feel insecure around you. We are all meant to shine, as children do . . . It is not just in some of us; it is in everyone and as we let our own light shine, we unconsciously give others permission to do the same. As we are liberated from our own fear, our presence automatically liberates others.

You can liberate others. You can make an impact on people if you just take action and do it. Think about how much more of an impact you can make if you first take care of your own affairs. Knowing your affairs are in order enables you to take even more action to grow your business and your wealth, which will enable you to help even more people and causes. Those people and causes then go out and help even more people and the cycle is stronger and more sustainable for generations to come. It just takes action.

Remember, behavioral finance tells us people won't take action until the pain they feel surpasses their personal threshold for dealing with that pain. That's their triggering event. The problem with wealth and estate planning is that much of the pain occurs after it's too late for a change in behavior to achieve the desired outcome. Quite often, the longer someone waits, the fewer options and flexibility are available to us to help them. With estate planning, you aren't the one who suffers. You've been promoted to the great beyond. You don't get to feel the pain; your heirs do. With some of the other planning that benefits you before you die, it is only you and your family who are going to be compromising their lifestyle due to procrastination.

Doing planning work is a responsibility, not an inconvenient option. Living a blessed life instills in us a responsibility to teach others and to be sure we do what we can to secure our future so we are not a burden on others. If we achieve an even higher level of success, our obligation takes on greater significance, because we are now in a position to provide for future generations in a prudent fashion. And for the 1% who have an opportunity to do all of those things and more, they have an opportunity to organize their affairs in a fashion that enables them to make a difference in their community as well. You see, wealth and estate planning are not just a nice thing to have; they're a must-have. Until you view this process as a must-have for yourself and your family, you will continue to procrastinate.

The best motivation is deciding to act. Get off your rear end and do your planning work. Plan your business and personal wealth, your estate and transition. You have ideas; write them down now, while they're still in your head. As I've mentioned, taking action requires some sort of triggering event. The triggering event could be a medical event for you, a family member, a friend, or a business partner that makes you step back and think about where you are and if you are doing everything you can to optimize and protect your wealth. A triggering event could be some event in your business, such as a merger or unsolicited offers you were not planning for previously. Things such as this may make you accelerate a planning process and move things forward sooner than expected. Life events such as marriages, divorces, deaths, and births could also cause a change in our mind-set, as if a switch was flipped that makes us take these things more seriously. I'd like to think this book is inching you closer and closer to taking action with every page you read. It all gets back to you finding and pursuing your unique purpose and then going for it.

For a complete tool kit so you can follow the path to not make the 7 Biggest Financial Mistakes, go to www.avoid7biggest.com.

INDEX

A

ACA (Affordable Care Act), 56, 130

advisors and advisor teams, 17–41, 204–5
  as architect/quarterback, 8–10, 27
  bonus online material, 40
  collaboration among, 24–26, 37
  communication with, 24–28
  complacency of, 18
  composition of teams, 22
  cost of, 30–31
  Entrepreneurial Ed and Edwina, 33–36
  fees, 36–37, 170–71
  friends and family as, 23–24
  as health care for businesses, 24
  holistic approach, 30, 35
  Internet as, 18
  lawyer specialization, 36
  nonspecialists as, 19–23, 162–63
  overcomplexity and oversimplification, 37–38
  selecting, 18

  self-assessment regarding, 38–40
  tax preparers versus, 28–32
  territorial nature of, 24, 27
  understanding you, your values and vision, 164–66
  working in silos, 24, 26

advisory boards, 108

affiliated service groups, 65

Affordable Care Act (ACA), 56, 130

aging, 35–36, 187

Aldridge, Irene, 148

alternative minimum tax (AMT), 82

America's Small Business Development Center, 104

Are You Ready? (EPI), 203–6

asset protection
  C corporations, 53–54
  cost to society, 132–34
  deductions, 96–97
  entity structuring, 45–51, 53–54, 66, 72–74
  health-care professionals, 178–79
  layers of protection, 134–37, 150

ABOUT THE AUTHOR

Bruce is as passionate about coaching successful entrepreneurs to avoid making mistakes in their personal finances as he is when coaching Little League. He educates on the dangers of the "conventional wisdom" of Wall Street! His blog topics are motivated by current or hot topics with regard to how to help the public build, protect, and manage their wealth around the dynamic current events of the world.

Bruce has extensive and comprehensive experience in finance, marketing, and operations, and has worked with companies of all sizes, from family owned to large corporations. His invaluable global experience allows him a qualified and specialized perspective on global business issues. Coupled with his experience, Bruce has earned an MBA with Honors from the EDHEC Business School in Nice, France, with an emphasis in International Business and Entrepreneurialism. He also earned a Certificate in Financial Planning from Golden Gate University.

Bruce's experience and education in international and domestic business gives him a specialized edge when working with real-estate investors, business professionals, and entrepreneurs, helping them make informed decisions regarding protecting and growing their wealth. His extensive knowledge of entity structuring, tax issues, employee and executive benefits, risk avoidance, and transition planning allows him to assist his clients with complex business planning. Rest assured, Bruce's primary goal and focus is to help his clients achieve an even greater impact on the people and causes they care about deeply.